The SAM Leader Survival Guide

A Practical Success Guide for Software Asset Management Professionals

Jim Hussey

ISBN 978-1-950647-43-9

Publisher's Cataloging-in-Publication data

Names: Hussey, Jim, author.
Title: The SAM leader survival guide : a practical success guide for software asset
management professionals / Jim Hussey.
Description: First trade paperback original edition. | Lakewood [Colorado] :
Technology Vendor Management Educational Services, 2020.
Identifiers: ISBN 978-1-950647-43-9
Subjects: LCSH: Information technology—Management. | Business enterprises—
Computer networks—Management.
BISAC: BUSINESS & ECONOMICS / Information Management.
Classification: LCC HD30.2 | DDC 658.4038—dc22

Cover background copyright Can Stock Photo / Andrey Kuzmin

Technology Vendor Management Educational Services

Publishing assistance by BookCrafters, Parker, Colorado.
www.bookcrafters.net

Table of Contents

Introduction

Like many of us in the software asset community, my involvement with SAM was thrust upon me with little planning or preparation. My organization had been through a series of audits with severe financial impact and the team assigned the responsibility to establish a software asset management operation was running months behind tool deployment and establishing the SAM operation. My assignment was to quickly fix the situation and get SAM functioning so the CIO could communicate to the CFO that Information Technology had successfully satisfied their commitment to better manage software as an asset and prevent future audits.

Little did I know this event was going to dramatically alter my professional life in such a profound manner. Very quickly, I found that I was the individual responsible for providing the CFO bi-weekly updates on non-compliance remediation efforts and continually working with IT finance and corporate accounting on accrual amounts. All this while I looked around to see my CIO, Senior Vice President of IT operations and VP of IT Infrastructure run for the doors and leave me standing alone to take the full brunt from the corporate executives. Not surprisingly, shortly after successful remediation of a 9-figure non-compliance, leadership decided to disband the SAM operation and myself with it.

Being a former journalist and researcher, I decided to study the SAM market. My initial goal was to learn if it was just my inexperience that led to the significant challenge I experienced or if SAM, as a discipline, suffers from the deep levels of dysfunction that I had personally experienced.

Since that time, I have dedicated the past four years to developing strategies and tactics to help SAM professionals achieve greater success and personal satisfaction. I consider myself a student of the software asset management community and every interaction I have is an opportunity to help all SAM professionals improve. With this thought top of mind, the concept of *The SAM Leader Survival Guide* was born.

The following pages are filled with the lessons I have learned through my own experience as a SAM leader of a Fortune 500 SAM operation utilizing a powerful SAM platform and a group of expert SAM analysts in addition to the experience of dozens of SAM professionals I interviewed who openly shared their thoughts and opinions to support best practice development. My hope is that the strategies described in this book, based upon the experiences and insight of these SAM professionals, will enable you to provide enhanced SAM performance and deliver quantifiable value.

Jim Hussey

SAM Evangelist

Acknowledgement

I would like to thank the Software Asset Management professionals who accepted my request for interviews and shared their insights so freely. The commitment I gave to them was that all who participated would be provided anonymity and I have kept that promise. The frustrations, challenges and opportunities you shared shaped the recommended tactics within *The SAM Leader Survival Guide*, producing a truly unique resource for the SAM community.

Of special note, I would like to thank my good friend Suresh Subbu whose support and ongoing encouragement helped me remain focused and complete this book. Suresh is the founder and CEO of Technology Vendor Management Educational Services (TVMES) and is my close colleague from our days in a corporate setting. I am proud to be part of the content development team for Suresh's sammaturity.com and support the mission he has established to help SAM professionals achieve greater professional success and job satisfaction.

Last, I must thank my wife Kim who has been very patient with me as I used my weekends to write *The SAM Leader Survival Guide*. In addition to sacrificing time on the weekends, she suffered through many, many discussions as the concepts outlined in this book took shape. I am confident if she ever decided to make a career change, she could step into a SAM leader role and excel!

Welcome

Hello and welcome to *The SAM Leader Survival Guide*. I am happy you're here as software asset management is a very important subject and one in which those who have contributed to this book have very real experience. As author of *The SAM Leader Survival Guide*, I have firsthand operational knowledge and experience of the good, the bad and the ugly of SAM operations and the challenges SAM leaders endure within an organization. To broaden the SAM perspective contained within the pages of this book, multiple SAM leaders were interviewed to learn their thoughts on the challenges and opportunities to establish effective SAM operations as well as their recommended best practices. *The SAM Leader Survival Guide* is a reference guide FOR SAM professionals BY SAM professionals. The individuals who contributed to this book know what is said behind closed doors when your discovery data uncovers a compliance challenge. We know leaderships response to this information and the expectation that SAM is accountable to chase down IT operational teams in an attempt to remediate.

The pages that follow have been structured as a reference guide. The goal is for you to refer to this document time and time again as you enhance and improve your software asset management operations. What we have found is organizations that take these preventative measures and proactively prepare their organization for a software audit, enjoy far greater performance and are viewed as more strategic contributors to the IT estate, ultimately securing survival of the SAM operation.

In many ways, the content that you're about to explore is truly unique in the software asset management space. There are wonderful associations such as the International Association of IT Asset Management (IAITAM) that educates the community on best practices across the software asset management lifecycle. There are powerful and effective advisory firms at the ready to help Software Asset Management leaders once an audit notification has been received or offer software asset management operational guidance to improve maturity. However, there are few resources that help SAM professionals deal with the dynamics and interpersonal requirements necessary for SAM operations to succeed on a day in, day out basis. *The SAM Leader Survival Guide* has been produced to fill this void.

Why do so many software asset management organizations suffer? Why do so many SAM leaders become expendable? The impact of the receipt of a software audit notification deals a crushing blow to our profession. If the SAM organization has not taking the necessary steps to prepare a cross functional team, SAM leaders face quick isolation and complete ownership and accountability of the outcome with limited or no actual authority. While Gartner and other firms do a wonderful job outlining the importance of an Audit Response Team (ART), *The SAM Leader Survival Guide* provides a step by step process to establish an ongoing, highly communicative strategy with cross-functional representatives on an ongoing basis. This proactive effort means when the ART is called into action, each member has clear, pre-defined accountability, responsibility and deliverables to support the activities necessary to execute a comprehensive, credible audit response.

The recommendations in the pages of this reference manual has been produced leveraging the extensive operational experience of a focused team of SAM professionals. The recommendations, guidance, and insights are not theoretical or academic. They are in fact based on real life lessons with the battle scars to prove it! Those who have contributed to this book have sat in your chair and held face to face meetings with CEOs, CFOs and CIOs at Fortune 500 companies concerning unbudgeted financial exposure due to license non-compliance. In fact, the concept of *The SAM Leader Survival Guide* came about because several of those that contributed to this effort, in addition to myself, did not survive these encounters. As we will cover shortly, many times, upon remediation of a software license, executives make the decision to eliminate a SAM function. *The SAM Leader Survival*

Guide has been designed to provide SAM professionals with a step by step reference guide to dramatically reduce this exposure and establish effective, productive, audit ready SAM operations.

Thank you again for making the investment to spend time to explore the SAM best practices you can implement to achieve greater success.

The SAM Leader Challenge: Setting the Stage

*T*he *SAM Leader Survival Guide*, while structured as a reference guide, is designed to be informal in style. We believe that the best way to bring forward the operational experience of the book's contributors, is to avoid consultant speak or executive speak and instead present the concepts in a grass-roots, operational manner. It is understood that each software asset management professional and each software asset management leader may not experience all or a portion of the items we describe in the following pages, however the recommendations remain the same. It is the actions described in the following sections that will produce the visibility, collaboration and teamwork necessary for software asset management professionals to not only survive audits but execute the software asset management lifecycle, bringing with it the efficiencies and optimizations we all believe possible from solid SAM operations.

10-Step SAM 'Death Dance'

When you look across the software asset management segment, the vast majority of organizations turn to their IT operations and infrastructure teams to execute SAM functions. Many times, the initial decision to invest in a SAM function has been the direct result of a software audit that had material financial impact. *The SAM Leader Survival Guide* asks why do so many CIOs and Chief Procurement Officers (CPOs) put so little dedicated focus and investment in a subject or area that has tremendous financial risk and operational disruption? How is it that Gartner and other leading advisory firms continually call out the focus of software publishers to drive revenue through an enhanced audit channel yet CIOs, CPOs and CFOs make minimal investments? While CIOs will identify effective management of software as an asset, they turn to IT operations or IT service management teams to own the SAM activity. Do CIOs not recognize the link between license non-compliance with poor deployment practices and appropriate controls typically owned by IT operations and IT service management?

Unfortunately, the below scenario plays out across organizations and their IT and Sourcing leadership time and time again. Many SAM professionals are very familiar with this progression and can easily predict the next step in what unfortunately can be referred to as a 'death dance'. *The SAM Leader Survival Guide* has been designed to help SAM leaders alter this course and redirect the focus down a positive path that produces value and intelligence that ultimately deliver tangible value. However, before we can implement these actions to alter the outcome, SAM leaders need to understand and anticipate the '10 Step SAM Death Dance'!

Step 1 – Audit Notification is received

Step 2 – CIO turns to Head of IT Infrastructure and ask 'Are we OK?'

Step 3 – Head of IT Infrastructure turns to IT Operations and ask 'Are we OK?'

Step 4 – IT Operations assures the Head of IT Infrastructure that there is no risk or issue. "We are good to proceed."

Step 5 – IT Operations deploys auditors scripts and provides requested discovery data to auditor with little to no validation or review.

Step 6 – Auditor produces multi-million-dollar Preliminary Enterprise License Position (ELP).

Step 7 – IT Operations claims auditors are wrong.

Step 8 – Procurement and IT attempt to negotiate a settlement.

Step 9 – Settlement achieved – Unbudgeted settlement or unneeded new products purchased.

Step 10 – Executives ask CIO, "what is the value of SAM?"

As SAM Leaders we need to look in the mirror and ask ourselves why does the above scenario continue to play out over and over again. Why is it that dedicated SAM operations are not more prevalent? Why is it despite writing checks for multi-million-dollar findings are organizations large and small not making an investment in SAM? Why are CIOs willing to continue to rely on the input of individuals who are stretched to perform their core job responsibilities such as IT operations or IT service management and expect them to be expert in the complexities of software use rights and compliance nuances?

The following pages have been designed to help SAM Leaders drive home the value of a dedicated SAM operation. Ultimately, it is the responsibility of SAM Leaders to demonstrate an investment in SAM produces a tremendous Return on Investment (RoI) while enabling operations to remain compliant and focused on delivery.

If this resonates with you, *The SAM Leader Survival Guide* will provide you the tools, techniques and activities necessary to establish and maintain SAM operations that deliver clear, bottom-line benefit.

Audit Storm Clouds Overhead

The challenge for SAM professionals is that we need to build solid SAM operations with the constant threat of storm clouds overhead. The continual focus in the press and from advisory firms around the growth of software audits, the use of software audits as a revenue stream by software publishers, and the horror stories around poor management around deployment of software assets have executives in the C-suite highly concerned. Despite this focus, the vast majority of organizations do not today have a true software asset management dedicated operation. Instead, corporate executives look to the procurement organization or the IT organization to take point if and when an audit arrives. Those tasked with interfacing with the auditors likely have little experience doing so and a full-time job that has them more than busy. From the outset, most firms grossly underestimate the impact of an audit in terms of time commitment, effort and potential financial exposure.

Ask yourself this basic question, 'when an audit notification arrives at your organization, who specifically will receive the physical notification and who will they hand responsibility to?' If you are unable to answer this quickly, there is an immediate gap. The unfortunate fact for SAM professionals, most executives when asked this question will give a blank stare. Typically, executives look at one another, perhaps identifying for the first time that there is a gap and a need to have a plan. In their defense, an audit notification triggers a strange internal dynamic. Strategic sourcing or procurement many times will lay claim to ownership and responsibility around the software publisher relationships, however when an audit notification arrives, they very quickly hand that responsibility to the senior most IT executive. In turn, the CIO looks to his or her organization to assign responsibility for owning the audit project and ultimate outcome.

What is most surprising about this dynamic is the fact that visibility of software audits is at an all-time high. Why are organizations so resistant to sit down and take proactive measures and plan? Why don't more organizations have dedicated SAM operations versus handing out functional sub-sets of SAM responsibilities to IT staff with no formal SAM training? *The SAM Leader Survival Guide* has been created to help SAM professionals establish the necessary visibility and create the required value to elevate SAM consistently to the strategic level deserved.

Executive View of SAM

It is important for us to take a few moments to look back and better understand why the software asset organization has been established. Many times, the software asset organization has been funded or created due to a previous audit finding that led to a highly visible financial impact. SAM leaders are continually surprised by the uphill battle encountered to implement a full software asset management capability that spans the full life cycle.

Unfortunately, it seems to take a nasty audit with a significant finding with severe financial impact that makes an organizations leader sit back and realize that their software asset is an exposure equal, in many ways, to the threat of cyber-attacks. Due to the experience of a failed audit with substantial non-compliance, CEO's, COO's and CFOs quickly sit the CIO down to demand answers to a very natural series of questions that ultimately leads to the creation of a software asset management organization.

- "What other software publishers do we have exposure?"

- "How do we prevent this from happening in the future?"

- "What are the policies or controls that need to be put in place to remove this risk?"

- "Is this really the best we can do to manage our software investment?"

In other words, *The SAM Leader Survival Guide* believes the typical process by which SAM organizations are created is a bottoms-up approach. What this means is that the strategic nature of a SAM operation, the value that it can produce for an organization in terms of efficiencies and optimizations, the insight on trends and consumption patterns, are never considered. It is truly focused on audit remediation.

Audit Insurance

Potentially the single most damaging perception for SAM leaders is the perception executives have that their investment in a SAM operation is in fact 'audit insurance'. The CIO's belief is they have budgeted for a dedicated SAM operation with an appropriate SAM platform which will prevent future audits. We have found few CIOs who view implementation of SAM operations as a truly strategic element to drive ongoing asset efficiency.

Hopefully this is not coming as a surprise to you. SAM leaders need to acknowledge this simple fact and develop the strategies and tactics to overcome this limited view of SAM's contribution. This Survival Guide has been developed to help SAM professionals implement a comprehensive set of activities that will firmly establish SAM operations as a valued contributor while establishing audit-ready operations.

CIO Anxiety: Audit = Lost Budget

Why would CIOs feel that the decision to invest in a SAM function is the equivalent of buying audit insurance? Audit findings and final settlements are unbudgeted events. These events force the CIO to brief the CFO and other corporate executives on an unplanned impact which tarnishes the reputation of IT. Additionally, CIOs and other technology leaders are constantly under pressure to reduce the cost associated with business as usual (BAU) operations. The direct benefit of a focus on cost reduction is the ability for CIOs to shift a larger percent of the IT budget to transformative undertakings such as digital proof of concepts (POC's) or test other emerging technologies. Audit findings not only impact the bottom line but impact the limited budget intended to help the CIO deliver on his or her overall business agenda.

SAM leaders need to proactively build the internal environment necessary to effectively build the cross-functional team for effective end to end software asset management engagement producing coordinated audit response. Audit ready organizations are able to focus on driving efficiency and optimization supporting the CIOs need to lower the cost of BAU operations, redirect budget to transformation and continually estimate software exposure and the associated tactics to remediate.

For SAM professionals the stakes are high. This is why *The SAM Leader Survival Guide* spends a great deal of time describing environment dynamics in order to identify the activities that can best counter unwanted, nonproductive activity limiting SAM contribution and ultimately SAM's perceived value. In essence, every dollar lost to an audit settlement is a dollar lost for transformation; which is the measuring stick for CIO effectiveness.

Is SAM a Function or Dedicated Discipline?

This is an extremely important decision made by CIOs at the outset. While the CIO has likely just experienced a negative audit outcome and they have committed to the executive team they will fix the issue and prevent future audit impacts, they turn to their leadership team for guidance. The challenge is this team likely does not themselves understand SAM and may in fact represent the root cause of the compliance challenge.

CIOs and Chief Procurement Officers who are tasked with building the function will quickly engage in the conversation about investment level and the appropriate staffing model to achieve the targeted outcome. In this point in the process, there has been little true discussion around the broader requirements. What tends to occur is the executive decision comes down to a basic question, 'Do I hire dedicated staff to perform the SAM function OR do I decompose SAM into its primary functions and assign these responsibilities to the IT teams best positioned to understand software issues?'

The above dynamic establishes a very dangerous precedent for software asset management professionals. SAM leaders typically find this decision has been made without the input of a SAM professional or perhaps individuals with interest to protect. Many times, it is the input of the IT head of infrastructure or IT operations leader who recommends SAM activities be assigned as a functional addition to their existing team. As SAM professionals, we understand the impact of this misconception which will become evident to the CIO when the next audit notification arrives.

The SAM Leader Survival Guide believes this to be a major challenge for SAM professionals as increasingly SAM is being viewed as an ITIL (Information Technology Infrastructure Library) or ISO (International Organization for Standardization) process do to the continued push of these international standard bodies to cover software asset management. More and more organizations are assigning SAM responsibility to IT Service Management (ITSM) teams with a potential addition of the SAM module to the ITSM platform. This dynamic will be covered in several other areas of this book; however, the core vision of this book is SAM leaders need to blend ITSM and SAM skills in order to meet expectations to effectively manage entitlements and accurate reconciliation against deployment date. Basically, it is a requirement to combine process and license management knowledge.

Managing Executive Expectation of SAM

Shortly we will dig into a number of techniques to help SAM leaders establish clear and realistic expectations with executives for SAM operations. It is an important item to note at this time as 'Setting the SAM Stage' requires a great deal of diligence on the part of SAM leaders to establish the appropriate environment or run the very real risk of suffering severe reputational damage before your SAM operations are fully functioning. Managing executive and CIO expectations are challenged by the fact that these expectations were defined prior to the SAM leader's arrival.

The SAM Leader Survival Guide refers to the period of time from when executives have communicated the decision to invest in a SAM function or dedicated operation to the point in time the platform is fully operational as the 'The Danger Zone'. During this period of time, SAM leaders need to be proactive to produce value and visibility of SAM's emerging capabilities. In addition to activities to compress this highly vulnerable period of time for SAM Leaders, Part 2, SAM Operational Execution, will provide multiple recommendations and tactics to deliver accelerated SAM value.

SAM Isolation

Understanding that SAM operations can quickly be isolated and viewed as a backroom, analytical function enables us as SAM leaders to develop targeted, proactive measures by which we can establish cross functional roles and responsibilities. In addition, SAM leaders can highlight the organization-wide implications of SAM processes, procedures, policies and controls necessary to integrate SAM accountability across the organization. Adherence to these policies, processes and controls will enable software asset professionals to better assess and identify those breakdowns that lead to potential compliance challenges. *The SAM Leader Survival Guide* outlines a number of very effective activities and processes by which SAM leaders can implement these remedies successfully, establishing a true cross-functional team understanding their roles and responsibilities in software compliance and audit support.

IT Operation 'Stone Wall'

Those who contributed to *The SAM Leader Survival Guide* were often asked, "What is the best or optimal reporting structure for a SAM leader and their organization?" It is our opinion, to be most effective, SAM Leaders need to report directly to the Chief Information Officer or the Chief Procurement Officer. This important alignment enables SAM professionals to function as an effective and objective contributor to enhancing a comprehensive view of IT operations and asset management implications. Unfortunately, the majority of the time, the SAM function or dedicated organization are a group of analysts assigned to a sub-team such as IT service management within IT operations.

At its core, the act of reconciling software discovery data against owned entitlements shines a spotlight on the effectiveness of software request, fulfillment, deployment and harvesting for rotation back to the license pool. This operational insight quickly identifies where process breakdowns occur, many of which are the responsibility of IT operations. Basically, when reporting into and a part of the IT operations team, SAM analysts quickly find themselves in a position where they are documenting the impact of fellow team member non-compliance. Additionally, this puts the IT operations leader in a position to report to their executive (likely head of IT Infrastructure who reports to the CIO) that their operation has contributed to an unbudgeted exposure.

As you would guess, in a significant portion of these scenarios, the information produced by SAM analysts does not successfully reach IT leadership and enable development of appropriate remediation plans. Many times, the unfortunate outcome is, when audited and served with a massive finding, IT operations quickly point to the inability of the SAM team to provide sufficient warning and remediation alternatives.

As SAM continues to grow in visibility, it is the hope of *The SAM Leader Survival Guide* that increasingly, SAM leaders are embraced by CIOs and CPOs as direct reports with the authority and accountability to fully execute the SAM agenda and deliver continuous value and intelligence. At the minimum, if the SAM function or dedicated SAM operation reports into IT operations, these individuals must allow SAM leaders to establish the necessary cross-organization visibility and awareness described in the upcoming Part 1 - Building a 'Sustainable' SAM operation.

Software Life-Cycle Disconnect

As Software Asset Management professionals, we fully appreciate the value of the full software lifecycle. Due to the fact that a SAM operation has been established for the sole purpose of audit protection, executives rarely understand the true value and extent of efficiency a well-run SAM organization can provide. While SAM professionals may be attempting to set up the necessary processes to support the lifecycle ranging from request to approve to purchase deploy manage upgrade and retire, leadership remains fixated on audit exposure. This is a key contributor to why so many CIOs do not establish SAM operations but choose to rely on infrastructure leaders and IT operations leaders as their software asset function.

However, SAM leaders need to carefully balance their description of a full SAM life-cycle and its many benefits with an understanding of the core value proposition critical to IT leadership. By doing so, SAM leaders have the opportunity to move from the generic SAM value proposition, which appears to have had limited success to date, and reinforce a broader agenda aligned to IT strategy. If not, executives quickly lose interest and attention to life-cycle benefit reporting.

In summary, as we bring 'The SAM Leader Challenge: Setting the Stage' section of *The SAM Leader Survival Guide* to a close, it is important for SAM leaders to reflect on the provided observations and identify which, if any, align with your specific experience. Why was your SAM operation initially funded? What is your reporting structure? Do you feel isolated or unable to escalate and drive the appropriate accountable parties? The following reference material is designed to help you successfully meet these challenged and more impacting SAM professionals.

The SAM Leader Survival Guide has been structured to serve as a reference manual designed for frequent use. Each section is described below, but the flow is intended to be basic, mirroring the logical progression from the decision point to enable a SAM function to those developments on the horizon promising to impact the world of SAM professionals in the not too distant future.

Part 1 – Building a 'Sustainable' SAM Operation provides SAM leaders the tools, tricks and techniques to establish the foundation necessary for SAM operations to achieve the promised value and contribution. While designed for a new SAM operation, the tactics described will help SAM leaders wherever they may be in terms of maturity.

Part 2 – SAM Organization & Operation Design covers the activities SAM leaders should employ as they select a SAM platform or service, design process alignment with upstream and downstream interfaces to enable SAM operations. Organization structure and the skills necessary to achieve SAM success brings this portion to a close.

Part 3 – SAM Operational Execution is a powerful guide for SAM leaders as they look to define their organization and operation while under pressure to achieve productivity. We will refer to a period of heightened exposure called The Danger Zone and describe the many activities SAM leaders can implement to reduce risk. Again, this section can be utilized at whatever point of maturity for the SAM function. The activities, tactics and recommendations in this portion of *The SAM Leader Survival Guide* also serve as remedies for challenges being experienced. Many times, the root cause of an issue or dynamic being experienced by a SAM leader can be remedied by application of the recommended strategies.

Part 4 – Audit Ready SAM Operations, as the 4th section of *The SAM Leader Survival Guide*, is intended to help SAM leaders establish the relationships and internal readiness in order to respond to an audit notification in a comprehensive, coordinated and rehearsed manner. The actions provided will help establish and maintain audit readiness while establishing the necessary linkage across the organization. A core component of this section will be SAM leaders establishing an ongoing team of peers, stakeholders and sponsors called the SAM Optimization Council, taking the concept of an Audit Response Team (ART) and creating ongoing, valuable alliances. We have purposely made this the 3rd part covered as to be effective, SAM leaders must have established the required foundation and clarity on operational execution BEFORE audit readiness can be established and maintained.

Part 5 – Internal Audit Dynamics: 'The Game Within the Game!' has been designed to help SAM leaders guide the internal Audit Response Team (ART) through the process of interaction with the auditor to achieve successful negotiations and settlement with proper audit closure proceedings.

Part 6 – Cloud: The Future is Here has been designed to help SAM leaders anticipate the unique dynamics that surround an organizations transformation to a digital platform utilizing cloud services. In the opinion of *The SAM Leader Survival Guide*, SAM leaders need to be proactive and get engaged with cloud issues or run the risk of being blindsided when issues emerge or simply become irrelevant.

Part 7 – On the Horizon briefly touches on two emerging technology trends that promise to have a significant impact on SAM leaders and ITAM professionals. As IT organizations continue to look for ways to increase agility and throughput, the concepts of 'Containers' and 'Serverless' computing present potential significant shifts in license consumption and usage metrics.

Part 8 – Pulling It All Together brings *The SAM Leader Survival Guide* to a close with some last-minute guidance and recommendations based upon your current state and typical challenges experienced by SAM operations.

So, on to building the foundation that enables your SAM organization to achieve success!

PART 1 – Building a 'SUSTAINABLE' SAM Operation

In order to establish an audit-ready SAM operation and the capability to maintain readiness, it is important to execute several basic activities to achieve organizational recognition that software asset management is far more than audit insurance, and the discipline of software asset management requires a broad, cross functional team. By achieving audit readiness, SAM professionals are able to minimize the typical scramble that occurs when an audit notification arrives and are able to focus a larger percent of SAM energies on effective execution of the full software asset lifecycle. By doing so, SAM professionals are able to document to leadership the value SAM delivers beyond audit avoidance. This enables SAM operations to address critical areas such as optimized renewals, effective retirement of assets along with utilization analysis delivering efficiency and intelligence.

By establishing audit readiness, SAM leaders reduce the classic feeling of walking on egg shells and waiting for the next audit notification to arrive. In many ways' organizations stick their heads in the sand and cross their fingers, praying an audit notification does not arrive in today's mail. In addition to being a complete waste of time, it endangers SAM professionals as they lose focus and are not able to execute the full SAM charter.

What is the root cause of the classic audit scramble? What are the things that can be done to minimize the focus on audits and maximize the focus on software productivity and optimization? We believe SAM leaders need to take the following structured steps to establish the foundation necessary to achieve audit readiness and execute a comprehensive SAM agenda. These recommendations have proven valuable time and time again as insight provided by *The SAM Leader Survival Guide* represents a summary of best practices for numerous SAM organizations. However, a word of caution regarding many of the elements you are about to review. It is very easy for you as a SAM professional, to view these recommendations as simple and perhaps even trivial. Without question, utilizing the items identified as SAM foundational elements will have significant benefit for your software asset organization. They will not only help you create and maintain audit readiness, more importantly, they will facilitate achieving alignment with your IT sponsors and stakeholders so your SAM operation can effectively execute the overall software asset charter.

SAM Foundational Elements

Sponsor Alignment

As mentioned previously, the vast majority of times we speak with CIOs or CPOs, our underlying observation is they have established a SAM function as a means to answer the difficult questions asked by the CEO. Unfortunately, what this means is, from the outset, SAM operations are compromised; vulnerable to the next burning platform that grabs executive attention.

In addition, as SAM leaders work across the organization, there is typically a lack of alignment with those leaders viewed as SAM program sponsors. This dynamic adds to confusion and misaligned expectations which in turn hastens the unraveling of intended SAM contribution. What this means is confusion and lack of alignment at the executive level and their direct reports immediately places SAM leaders in a challenged position to execute.

The SAM Leader Survival Guide continues to observe SAM leaders don't look beyond their direct reporting structure to assess those key executives who have a potential high degree of influence over how others in the organization view SAM. It is critical that SAM leaders look beyond their direct manager and reporting structure to fully comprehend those key executives who have direct influence over SAM's perceived value. *The SAM Leader Survival Guide* has categorized three unique types of executive sponsors SAM leaders need to carefully identify and develop a game plan to engage, educate and gain their support.

Sustaining Sponsor

The individual the SAM leader reports to directly may not fully understand the goals and objectives of a solid software asset management life cycle. They may have recently been assigned the task of building the SAM function but likely have no direct experience with SAM issues or knowledge of core SAM principles. Ideally a direct report to the CIO, the Sustaining Sponsor must clearly understand and agree with the mission, charter and intended value to be delivered by SAM operations.

While this is the ideal scenario, the majority of SAM operations report into one of the following structures, each having benefits and challenges.

IT Infrastructure

In many situations, the 'Sustaining Sponsor' may In fact also be the leader of an operational area that in fact is a core contributor to compliance challenges and process breakdowns. In this scenario, the ability for SAM operations to communicate findings can be severely limited.

IT Service Management

Perhaps due to the success of Service Now as a SAM platform or the expansion of SAM process definition in ITILv4 or ISO standards, increasingly SAM operations are being folded into ITSM teams with accountability assigned as a process. In this scenario, the 'Sustaining Sponsor' likely has limited knowledge of entitlement management challenges and the requirement for effective upgrade and downgrade revisions to maintain accuracy.

Vendor Management

Many executives view the threat of a software audit as a vendor management issue. By aligning SAM operations within the VMO, the perceived benefit is those that are expert in managing vendors should also be capable of effectively managing the software estate, software publishers and successfully manage audits. The challenge here with this scenario is that VMO and SAM operational teams speak a very different language. In addition, the VMO is challenged to exert the needed leverage and drive the required accountability across IT operations. If the VMO leader directly reports to the CIO and the below items of SAM Mission Statement, Value Statement and Rules of Engagement (RoE) have been addressed successfully, this scenario works well.

Procurement/Sourcing Office

As Sourcing owns contract negotiations and potentially maintains the currency of license entitlements, SAM operations can be aligned within this organization. When reporting into Sourcing, SAM operations can be challenged when trying to outline deployment breakdowns and drive required remediation actions as they can be viewed more as internal audit more than a solution provider.

Executive Sponsor

The Executive Sponsor is the individual the Sustaining Sponsor Reports to. The desired outcome is if the SAM leader is not a direct report to the CIO then the Sustaining Sponsor is a direct report to the CIO. Ultimately, it is the Executive Sponsor who will be the senior most executive to communicate the SAM mission, value, and required operational rules of engagement (RoE) for SAM to be successful.

SAM leaders need to be careful, when developing a relationship with the Executive Sponsor, not to appear as if they are going around the Sustaining Sponsor or attempting to undermine the Sustaining Sponsors authority. Ideally, SAM leaders will meet with both to facilitate collaboration and develop a joint vision of SAM's expectations and charter.

Peripheral Sponsor

There are multiple other executives that can prove of great value to SAM leaders. If managed properly, these key executives will help extend the reach and influence of SAM into critical areas such as IT Finance, Information Security, Purchasing and Legal.

IT Finance may be the primary beneficiary of an effective SAM program. SAM leaders need to understand the reporting produced by IT finance and how the massive volume of data SAM operations produces can be aligned to best support IT finance's needs. Software spending by publisher, renewal schedules, anticipated growth or true-up impacts etc. typically are items IT finance will approach Sourcing IT category managers and may not think to approach SAM. SAM professionals need to establish their value to IT finance and should have the answers covering consumption rate, forecasting, versions owned vs. versions implemented, and compliance gaps at the ready whenever IT finance requests.

A close second to the importance of a good partnership with IT finance is for the SAM leader to develop strong alignment with Information Security (InfoSec) leadership. In many ways, an effective SAM operation provides valuable information for InfoSec to better identify vulnerabilities as well as process breakdowns (patch management). As InfoSec carries a great deal of internal clout, when combined with IT finance, SAM leaders have established highly critical and valuable relationships.

As you read thru *The SAM Leader Survival Guide*, please keep this very important concept top of mind. When the CIO has just had a budget cut and needs to identify areas to target reductions, the goal of SAM leaders is to have the CIO, InfoSec leadership (perhaps the CISO) and IT Finance view SAM as too valuable a strategic contributor to impact. This can only come about by developing insight of what is important to these leaders and proactivity delivering the information they need to be effective.

Stakeholder Engagement

The SAM Leader Survival Guide defines a Stakeholder as the 'peers' to the Sustaining Sponsor. Many times, these individuals will rely on 'cascade' communications from the CIO versus proactively delivering the message to their teams. As we describe below, working through these Stakeholders to effectively reach their team leaders is key to securing SAM support. SAM leaders need to sit with their Sustaining Sponsor and outline the value of developing close relationships with his or her peers. Again, based on the dynamics within your organization, meeting with your direct reports peers could be interpreted as politically motivated.

SAM leaders need to consider an additional dimension to building relationships with the Sustaining Sponsors peers. In many organizations, the targeted Stakeholders may in fact lead a team that contributes heavily to license non-compliance due to poor deployment or process adherence. Before sitting with these individuals, SAM leaders need to assess the potential challenges and shape the conversation accordingly.

SAM Mission Statement

The SAM Leader Survival Guide recognizes that this is an elementary item, however it is shocking to see the number of SAM leaders who ignore or underestimate the value in creating their SAM Mission Statement or miss the opportunity for natural collaboration across the organization. As an advisor supporting SAM leaders, one of the first items requested is a copy of the current SAM Mission Statement. Not surprisingly, SAM leaders rarely produce a documented Mission Statement. What is shared by SAM leaders is that they have discussed the subject with the executive sponsor and there is alignment. What quickly becomes apparent when the same discussion is had with IT, sourcing or finance executives, is that there is little alignment, leading to a wide variety of expectations and assumptions ultimately putting SAM operations at risk. This fundamental disconnect has a profound impact on how a SAM operation is viewed and the ability to be a strategic asset to IT, Sourcing and IT finance.

Why is something so basic a cornerstone of a Software Asset Management operation such a challenge? In many ways, the challenge rests with the root cause or the event that initiated focus on establishing a SAM capability in the first place. As previously discussed, the majority of SAM operations were formed due to a negative audit outcome. Rarely do the executives consider the additional elements a productive SAM operation can provide the organization.

Unfortunately for the SAM leader, if not careful, their success will be tied to 'discovery data' and SAM tool coverage versus taking the time to establish and gain agreement across key executives of the comprehensive SAM Mission Statement. *The SAM Leader Survival Guide* will address the dynamic experienced by many SAM operations of being viewed as a 'backroom' function in Part 2 – SAM Operational Execution. For SAM leaders, while the team is busily initiating activities to establish a new SAM operation or those SAM leaders who have inherited a new operation, taking the time to craft the SAM Mission Statement with the participation and input across a broad range of executives and leaders is invaluable.

For those SAM leaders who do have a documented SAM Mission Statement, it is important to continually review and update in order to remain current with operational dynamics. In Part 5 - Cloud: The Future is Here, *The SAM Leader Survival Guide* suggests tactics SAM leaders can execute to pull cloud governance elements formally into SAM scope and accountability.

Executive Sponsor Validation Session – Mission Statement Development
SAM leaders have the opportunity to engage executives in a focused conversation to explore what the key drivers are for that individual while helping educate them on the extended value SAM can provide. This may take SAM professionals out of their comfort zone, but it will show that while we as SAM professionals like to talk about entitlements, license metrics and reconciliation, executives want to anticipate and remediate risk and impacts. Bringing this dynamic into alignment sets the stage for SAM operations to achieve strategic status.

Step 1 - Carefully consider 'all' executives who provide valuable sponsorship for SAM operations. While there will clearly be an IT executive - hopefully the CIO directly – there can be other important sponsors who can influence the visibility and value of the SAM mission. Many times, this includes IT Finance, Information Security (InfoSec), IT Sourcing category manager or Chief Procurement Officer, IT Infrastructure leader and Vendor Management leader.

Step 2 - Working across the identified parties, hold a series of individual focused discussions during which the value and benefit of the full SAM life cycle is discussed. In addition, be sure to define the level of support each cross-functional team needs to provide in order to achieve effective software management.

Step 3 - Document the key areas of focus, metrics and objectives of each individual as this will help form the basis for SAM reporting and communications.

Step 4 - Gain concurrence, insight and validation of the key items by continually updating a brief 'mission statement' to form the foundation of the meeting and identify the tactics and measurements by which the SAM mission will be measured.

Step 5 - Gain acknowledgment that visible support will be required to continually reinforce adherence to the controls and processes across the identified parties.

SAM leaders need to be careful not to assume there is only a single executive sponsor who influences the decision to maintain and invest in SAM operations. Utilize the above approach for all categories of 'Sponsors' including the Executive Sponsor, Sustaining Sponsor and Peripheral Sponsors. Researching the needs of each functional area and the leader's expectations of SAM operations is critical to establishing a comprehensive SAM Mission Statement that addresses broader corporate needs.

Once a core SAM Mission Statement has been developed, based on these interactions and input of the identified sponsors, SAM leaders need to turn their attention to the stakeholders who will ultimately determine the success of the software asset management operation.

Stakeholder Sessions – Mission Statement Education

Stakeholders are a difficult group for SAM leaders to achieve and maintain alignment. The reason this proves to be a political challenge is a comprehensive SAM Mission Statement runs the very real risk of drawing attention to areas of process breakdown these stakeholders are responsible for. These breakdowns contribute to potential unbudgeted exposure.

The ideal scenario is for the CIO to deliver a very powerful and clear message on the agreed SAM Mission Statement. By doing so, operational stakeholders – typically those individuals who can undermine SAM effectiveness through passive-aggressive behavior or outright resistance – are put on notice.

The goal would be to have the CIO direct reports arrange to have each of their teams participate along with key members from the 3rd layer (direct to a direct to the CIO). Many times, these are the individuals who actually control operational execution and intended communications utilizing the 'cascade' model which has little value. In these sessions, the idea is to identify the need for smaller, operation specific meetings to review roles and responsibilities and align expectations. In these sessions it is always a good idea to review typical scenarios for the specific team with the likely outcome and impact for non-compliance.

Mission Statement Outcome: Responsibility Vs Accountability

Executing the above SAM Mission Statement model produces a predictable chain of events. Executed properly, teams that have been successful in avoiding any real accountability for non-compliance due to process breakdown begin to realize SAM operations is going to monitor and identify and control and process noncompliance and associated potential exposure. *The SAM Leader Survival Guide* has found these individuals are typically targeted to be members of the Audit Response Team

(ART), but if SAM does not properly nurture the relationship, these individuals will sit back and say 'let me know if I can be of any help!'. In Part 3 – Audit Ready SAM Operations, the concept of the SAM Optimization Council is defined for SAM leaders to form an extended internal advisory team with an ongoing role in supporting SAM operations. This moves operational level managers from declaring independence of any responsibility to being fully engaged with clearly defined responsibility and accountability in support of SAM operations.

With the development of a clear SAM Mission Statement that is endorsed by IT leadership with accountability identified, SAM leaders can successfully drive software asset responsibility and accountability to the cross-functional IT, Sourcing, Procurement and Vendor Management teams.

We're not done! The SAM Mission Statement must be supported by a separate and equally critical platform for SAM leaders. The SAM Value Statement must address the broader, cross-functional aspect of not only software asset, but the insight SAM professionals have on IT efficiency and optimization.

SAM Value Statement

A SAM Mission Statement alone is not enough. In the case of Software Asset Management operations, much like the requirements for Vendor Management or Third-Party Risk Management organizations, leaders must be able to demonstrate clear linkage with direct business outcomes producing identifiable value. Risk avoidance or 'save' is simply not enough to ensure the ongoing viability of SAM operations. Traditionally SAM leaders rely on describing the software asset management life cycle and reduction in annual software spend as the primary value produced by SAM operations. Unfortunately, IT executives and IT finance, who according to Gartner see an annual average growth of 7-9% in software spend, view SAM's position on software save as an empty, non-material item. This leads IT executives to underestimating the value they are realizing from SAM operations and increases the vulnerability for this team when budgets are tight and IT leaders are being pressed to deliver more with less.

Utilizing insight gained through development of the SAM Mission Statement, SAM Leaders must develop a second and perhaps even more critical communication concerning the benefit of their organization and contribution to business strategy and objectives. This must be made in a clear statement defining value delivered by SAM operations including the manner in which this identified value is delivered and associated metrics by which achievement is measured.

The lack of a clearly defined SAM Mission Statement, combined with the inability of SAM leaders to articulate and document value delivered, ultimately leads to the decision by IT executives to disband a dedicated SAM function. Like technology vendor management organizations (VMO), without a true appreciation for the benefits realized by SAM or VMO's and an appreciation of the skills necessary to execute these disciplines, IT leaders quickly assign responsibility to IT operations, assign functional elements to existing team members and repurpose the funding previously consumed by SAM operations.

To avoid this dynamic, SAM leaders need to look deeper at the intelligence they can generate. Evaluate this data from multiple perspectives in order to identify areas for IT efficiency and optimization. Based on the level of detail available to SAM professionals through ongoing SAM discovery, we have a unique perspective into multiple areas that form the essence of IT 'business as usual' (BAU) operations. Careful analysis and interpretation of the data within each of these areas can yield incremental insight delivering potential value to IT operations. These process areas include:

IT Service Management

The goal of an ITSM system is to form the foundation and repository of all IT operation activity. This covers incident management as well as asset request across a broad range of areas, several of which are key for SAM operations to maintain a close eye on. The ITSM platform should be integrated with purchasing so once approvals are granted, based upon the required level of permissions or signing authority, the action requested is recorded and memorialized.

For SAM professionals, close involvement in the IT change management process is critical, particularly those changes that impact software licensing rules such as increased core allocations needed for improved operational performance or other changes driven by new releases into the environment. If there are rogue devices and software installs appearing in discovery data, this is an indication of ITSM non-compliance which could be an indication of increased risk and vulnerability in the environment. Careful review and reporting of IT change management analysis brings increased discipline and focus to IT operations and enhanced IT financial management as rogue devices can be quickly identified and assigned to the appropriate cost center.

ITIL Process Adherence & Participation

In many ways, effective SAM operations are directly impacted by the level of process adherence across IT operations. Core ITIL (Information Technology Infrastructure Library) process areas including Change Management, Configuration Management, Patch Management and Release Management are an essential indicator of process discipline. Deployment Management is an additional area where SAM professionals need to function as a critical checkpoint as it is surprisingly common for infrastructure teams to secure approval of a 'standard edition' license and then deploy an 'enterprise edition' or another higher edition.

SAM leaders need to ensure SAM operations has representation in each of the core IT operations and ITIL status meetings to ensure potential software impact is considered when changes in the environment are being considered. SAM operations are then able to act as an independent function to offer recommendations for improved ITIL alignment and performance leading to efficiency and reduced vulnerabilities.

The SAM Leader Survival Guide mentions in several places the current dynamic that IT Service Management (ITSM) teams are increasingly being identified by IT executives as the organization and professionals best positioned to assume SAM responsibility. While this can easily be viewed as a natural extension of responsibility and endorsed by IT operation and infrastructure leadership, it is the opinion of *The SAM Leader Survival Guide* that a team of ITSM associates requires the addition of true SAM professionals to effectively perform software asset management task.

Information Security

SAM leaders should have an excellent relationship with Cybersecurity and Information Security leaders. While developing the SAM Mission Statement and engaging with leaders in these disciplines, SAM leaders need to identify the data most valued and determine how SAM operations can deliver. Areas such as the timely status of Patch Management with the associated implementation information can be of value. While this may not be a save, SAM operations are contributing to more effective InfoSec.

An additional area SAM leader can provide value is to track accuracy of Active Directors and identification of 'unused assets' assisting in proper disposal and removal of potential vulnerabilities.

Project Management – 'Move to Production'

Many errors in terms of sizing and estimating software cost for net new projects lead quickly to non-compliance or poor license utilization. Most Project Management methodologies have a life cycle that progress the level of budget accuracy from +/- 50% to +/- 10% as the team moves from high level design to detailed design based on final requirements. It is important for SAM leaders to participate in each stage as they can quickly support any software estimates and guide the team to the correct version and core processor requirements.

Having insight to the flow of upcoming projects provides SAM the ability to report to leadership the alignment of software to BAU activities and transformation programs. Combined with the raw purchase data, SAM can produce a valuable picture for CIOs on the pace at which the organization is transforming, the alignment of the purchased software with software strategy and effectiveness of initial estimates compared to final actuals.

Application Rationalization

Application teams will justify implementation of a new platform or movement to a cloud environment identifying the elimination of the original environment or redundant applications. While used in the business case for justification, rarely is the closure of the legacy environment tracked effectively and removed from service. SAM leaders have the opportunity to document the cost of multiple applications performing the same task, time to application shutdown as well as those applications yet to be terminated.

IT Asset Utilization

This is an area that has become a real opportunity for SAM leaders as contract structure and virtualization have changed the landscape. Many SAM leaders and their team members are challenged to maintain accurate compliance profiles. The issue typically centers on a change in license metrics such as a conversion from 'processor to core'.

As discussed above, the SAM team needs to be embedded in most of the IT operation process areas to ensure alignment with license requirements. Typically, a change to production environment such as a move to a new virtual or physical box will be covered in the change management process. It is very challenging for IT teams to remain current on all the changes and variances between software publishers. Having SAM represented in these sessions helps everyone involved.

A change in core count can have a major impact to compliance and have a dramatic algorithmic impact to license consumption. SAM leaders need to carefully study utilization of core and processor levels to identify potential targets for reduction in data center or cloud footprint. This information not only enables SAM to challenge environment decisions to reduce software impact, but it also is an indicator of overall environment utilization.

In essence, SAM professionals, through careful reporting and analysis, can become a strategic partner in Business as Usual (BAU) optimization. In addition, as most organizations are aggressively moving to the cloud, SAM leaders can help identify processor utilization before the cloud environment is ordered and workload moved.

Cloud Consumption Management

Part 6 of *The SAM Leader Survival Guide* takes a more detailed look at this significant opportunity for SAM professionals to provide IT executives value. Cloud consumption, while an emerging governance discipline, is not intended to focus on architecture adherence. This is typically the reasonability of the Cloud Center of Excellence (CCOE). SAM leaders can deliver strategic value by helping CIOs monitor cost of cloud assets that are being under-utilized or essentially sitting idle; Gartner refers to this as 'toxic' consumption.

We have spent a significant amount of time in this section identifying different areas where SAM leaders have the potential to document tangible value for IT executives. While every organization is different, many of these elements will be similar and provide excellent points of discussion with sponsors and stakeholders. By virtue of simply having these discussions, SAM leaders stand to shift the perception of SAM operations in a positive manner. Our recommendation is to select those items that offer the best alignment with your corporate objectives and evolve the manner in which SAM measures and reports the analysis. Don't attempt to implement all of the value metrics at once as you run the risk of overreaching. Identify those most strategic, establish the baseline and foundation for several months, and then expand to the second layer or grouping. The intent of this section on developing a strategic SAM Value Statement in support of the SAM Mission Statement is to demonstrate understanding of IT operations and the challenges encountered by IT executives and, in particular, IT finance. This not only solidifies SAM operational 'survival', but elevates the contribution made to achieving stated goals.

SAM Foundation Extension
Software Publisher 'Rules of Engagement'

We have found SAM leaders hesitant to push the issue of 'Rules of Engagement' despite the risk associated with poor or improper interaction with software publisher representatives. Perhaps it has to do with reporting structure or where the SAM leader is typically 'leveled' within the IT organization, but lack of focus on developing and communicating clearly defined Software Publisher Rules of Engagement (RoE) continues to cost organizations staggering amounts of unbudgeted cost.

This is slightly different from the challenge encountered by leaders of IT Vendor Management organizations (VMO). Many software publisher account teams, implementation and service team members will 'offer' a client's technology team to optimize the software installed for efficiency and better performance. If the internal IT operations team is not made aware of this potential issue, educated on the impacts and informed of the consequence of enabling a software publisher account team to receive environment reports, organizations have exposure.

With development of the SAM Mission Statement, SAM Value Statement and working proactively across the sponsor and stakeholder landscape, SAM leaders need to make certain clearly defined Rules of Engagement (RoE) are defined and agreed. SAM RoE should address multiple dimensions as software publisher teams will continually probe to find openings.

Subjects to Avoid

Software Publisher account teams and implementation teams are all compensated to some degree on revenue of a client. That means they are continually looking for sales opportunities and 'up-sell' potential. Unfortunately, if a client is not expanding as the account team has forecast, an audit judgement can be used as a bargaining chip to secure incremental sales.

When speaking with the account manager or any representative, IT operations, IT finance, Sourcing and business leaders need to be careful not to share information that can put the company at a disadvantage. Subjects such as upcoming transformation programs, expansion with competitive technologies or movement to a competitive cloud service provider (CSP) indicate to an account team that the percent of customer will be reduced.

Activities to Avoid

We have all become very comfortable with the benefits of a virtual workplace. Technologies such as WebEx, Zoom, Teams and many others have led to great productivity and reduced lost time. However, IT teams need to be coached on the dangers of doing 'screen share' sessions with a software publisher' representative. Many times, as a technical resource jumps between views, the potential of the person viewing the screens quickly seeing items indicating deployment breakdown leading to potential exposure if audited. Without question, these observations are funneled back to the account team and there are internal discussions at the software publisher on how best to proceed.

Script Avoidance

A clear message needs to be communicated by the IT executive office pertaining to the consequence of an employee running an unauthorized script on behalf of the software publisher and providing the output to that account team. The number of times this action leads to significant financial consequence is truly staggering, yet those individuals who enabled the event rarely face consequence. Instead, the SAM operation appears to absorb the brunt.

SAM leaders need to be very proactive on this RoE and continually educate IT teams of the tactics typically employed by account teams and the consequence. We have observed firms create policy stating that if not adhered to, the consequence will be immediate termination for cause. While this is rare, the importance of the issue is made clear.

'Policy to Operations' Bridge

Develop your SAM RoE portfolio to form an important link between SAM Policy that has been approved by executive leadership and the operational realities of managing software assets. If the general SAM Policy is generic and lacking accountability and consequence, SAM RoE need to be made more robust with specificity of the issues, challenges and impacts.

SAM Executive Steering Committee

We will reference the importance and use of the SAM Executive Steering Committee (Exec. SteerCo) multiple times. As we move to completing the recommended activities to establish a sustainable SAM operation, the Exec. SteerCo will be an important group of targeted individuals to provide support and manage expectations across the organization.

It is important to identify those sponsors and stakeholders most influential as well as key operational leaders who will directly influence the ability to implement SAM operations. This includes individuals such as IT Finance, Chief Information Security Officer or Information Security, IT Operations, Privacy, Risk, IT Operations and Service Management and Network functions. This establishes a core group of SAM Leaders to ensure they are fully informed on all developments, timing and challenges. We recommend formal, every other month meetings during implementation and establishing formal SAM operations. It is suggested the frequency of Exec. SteerCo meetings move to quarterly and ultimately settling in at a rhythm of semi-annual. Content for these meetings will take shape in the following pages, but should ensure a high degree of focus on trends, analysis and recommended actions with identified consequence if recommendations are ignored. Remember, the process of establishing the SAM Mission Statement and the SAM Value Statement has prepared SAM leaders to determine the most appropriate information for Exec. SteerCo members and the manner in which they are communicated.

SAM – IT Operations Alignment

With the visible and active support of SAM's executive sponsors and stakeholders combined with clearly defined Rules of Engagement, SAM leaders need to personally drive this message throughout IT operations. As mentioned in the 'Setting the Stage' section, IT operations can be a particularly challenging group to secure proactive and ongoing support. Even with SAM leaders being a direct report to the CIO or CPO, SAM leaders and their team members benefit from good knowledge of IT operations. Having this insight enables SAM teams to accurately draw the lines of accountability between SAM functions and IT operations.

A natural area of potential friction with IT operations and IT service management is the subject of who owns the Configuration Management Database (CMDB). Having a firm understanding of the roles and responsivities for all parties is necessary to ensure SAM leaders suddenly don't become the owner of this important but challenging area. Many IT organizations will quickly point to the SAM platform as the de facto CMDB. SAM leaders need to tread carefully in this area.

SAM Policy Development and Management

You may be surprised *The SAM Leader Survival Guide* views SAM Policy as the fourth area critical to building a strong, successful SAM operation. As policy is seen as the initial step or life cycle activity, the suggestion for SAM leaders is unless the previous conditions are in place, whatever SAM polices are developed, they will have minimal effect.

Software asset management, as a discipline, continues to expand and evolve. To remain current, SAM leaders need to consider development of multiple SAM Policy statements to address scenarios by which software assets can be secured and sensitive to the role of individuals. In essence, the trend is for SAM leaders to develop a targeted, small portfolio of perhaps 3 levels of SAM Policy dependent on the individual's role. This includes:

- General, Corporate-wide Software Policy

- Cloud Use Policy

- SAM Accountability for IT Organization – Life Cycle Management

- SAM Internal Proprietary Information Protection

- SAM Accountability for Software Deployment & Disposal

Combined with the previous actions recommended in this section, creating a series of SAM Policies reinforces the seriousness in which Corporate and IT executives view software as an asset.

SAM Control Development and Management

Software Asset Management Controls go hand in hand with defined SAM policy and SAM alignment with core IT process. The intent of defining SAM Controls is to anticipate where natural breakdowns occur in the life cycle of the software asset. In Part 4 – Audit Ready SAM Operations, the concept of the SAM Optimization Council will be discussed. An important element of this extended group is to continually monitor and report control effectiveness. In this manner, SAM leaders are able to shine a light on control deficiencies, the impact of non-compliance and collaborate on mitigation actions.

Software Request Controls

Breakdown or inefficiencies in controls related to the request and acquisition of software may not become fully evident until a team is in the midst of an audit response. There are multiple dynamics which can cause challenges to reconcile deployed software against license entitlements. It is critical that SAM leaders establish controls covering the process by which software is requested, order fulfillment and deployment aligned with the approved software.

The concept of 'signing authority', centralized purchase authority, limited approvers, the number of purchase channels all need to be defined with IT executives and SAM's sponsors and stakeholders. The goal is to improve coordination while at the same time introduce accountability. Once defined and aligned to the SAM Policy Statements, SAM leaders need to anticipate the manner in which breakdowns can be identified with non-compliance challenged. There are times where effective reporting and analysis of these items will drive the desired behavior. If this fails, then develop the formal control.

Software Deployment Controls

In the area of software deployment, SAM leaders rely heavily on IT operations ITIL process discipline including change, configuration and release management. This is critical as SAM leaders need to link the 'requested' license type with the 'deployed' license type to ensure alignment. Not surprisingly, when SAM leverages the discovery platform to scan the environment or engages a 3rd party to conduct a license baseline, a consistent 'control' breakdown is the deployment of a higher version or edition than the requested license. This leads to rapid non-compliance.

An additional 'control' for SAM leaders to monitor is the platform software is deployed on. Whether virtual or physical, the software needs to be installed in an environment consistent with the business case number of core processors or virtual CPU's.

Lastly, individuals should be prevented from downloading software on their workstations by tight control of administrator rights. This can be managed using the ITSM ticketing and request system and any exceptions can be quickly identified.

Software Reclamation

SAM diligence must be applied across the full software life cycle in coordination with IT Asset Management and IT operations. As systems and compute assets are decommissioned, they must be scrubbed to reclaim software licenses for future assignment. *The SAM Leader Survival Guide* continues to observe firms encounter sever challenges maintaining devices and users in Active Directory, an indication that assets are not promptly removed or decommissioned, wiped and removed from maintenance inventory.

While harvesting and reuse of software assets is an important SAM life cycle activity, SAM leaders need to leverage the insight gained in this area as this is an indication of the discipline of IT operations. This is an important aspect to help drive SAM's contribution to value and should be viewed as a strategic IT contributor.

Building a Sustainable SAM Operation Summary

We have spent a great deal of time sharing with you the preceding steps to establish the foundation necessary for a strategic SAM operation. We have observed time and time again that SAM leaders who have not taken the time to consider these simple measures encounter significant headwinds to have SAM operations viewed as a strategic capability versus audit insurance or a simple back office analyst function. By taking these proactive measures, SAM leaders have effectively cemented the comprehensive benefits software asset management can provide IT leaders.

You may be wondering why we have focused on these activities grouped to build a sustainable SAM operation before discussing SAM tools, organization alternatives or SAM skills. The reason is, unless SAM leaders take the recommended actions and fully understand expectations across stakeholders and sponsors, whatever SAM tool is selected or organization structure employed will struggle. Conversely, with the above recommendations carried out, SAM leaders are now fully prepared to develop the appropriate organization to align with expectations.

With clarity on SAM policy, controls, process alignment, value and mission statements and alignment with IT operations, a SAM leader has in essence developed the requirements for a SAM platform as well as a directional understanding of the organization structure. This has enabled the SAM leader to avoid the typical rush to select a tool prior to overall strategy development. Sequencing SAM strategy development and defining the operational game plan before engaging in the technology selection allows SAM leaders to more accurately define tool or platform selection with clear alignment to intended operations. As we are about to see, there are many technology choices and solutions to consider. Having our foundation firmly established will enable us to quickly align technology alternatives with operational expectations.

Part 2 - SAM Organization & Operation Design

We are now ready to begin the process of developing the organization necessary to deliver on the agreed SAM mission. Utilizing the consensus achieved as we established the foundation, SAM leaders must now turn their attention to defining the elements necessary to deliver on their mission. A critical portion of the SAM business case will be development of a comprehensive budget that accurately defines the investment necessary to deliver the SAM mission and value collaboratively established with sponsors and stakeholders.

A word of caution: Effective SAM operations will require more than 'a guy and a tool'. Unfortunately, when SAM leaders are under pressure to achieve unrealistic expectations established by executives, this error occurs time and time again. The root cause being the lack of engaging IT leadership in any of the activities covered previously. SAM leaders succumb to the pressure from IT leadership to communicate to corporate executives they have taken action to mitigate audit exposure. As we are about to see, there is a great deal SAM leaders must consider from the outset. *The SAM Leader Survival Guide*, understanding this pressure, explores the activities necessary to evaluate the appropriate SAM reporting tool first. This will enable SAM leaders to establish a communications channel back to the SAM Exec. SteerCo and keep them informed on progress.

Platform Selection

There are a number of important factors to consider prior to engaging the many software asset management market participants providing some form of software asset management capability. Currently none of the SAM market participants enjoy a dominant position, producing a somewhat scattered and confused array of choices. However, there are steps we can take as SAM leaders to reduce the number of alternatives to consider and hone in on an appropriate solution for your specific environment.

SAM leaders need to engage in the platform selection process with eyes wide-open. In the experience of *The SAM Leader Survival Guide* there is no single SAM platform that will provide 100% accuracy. SAM leaders need to understand the SAM platform, if implemented properly, will be 80-85% effective. It is still advisable to have the SAM team execute system generated reports on a scheduled basis to evaluate areas where challenges may occur. RVTools, MSDN, Active Directory, SCCM are examples of reports that will help SAM professionals assess the accuracy of their selected platform and identify potential calibration opportunities to improve accuracy.

Software Estate Considerations

Not all organization software estates are created equal. Understanding a few key factors will point SAM leaders toward those tools, platforms or managed service best aligned to meet the specific needs of the current environment.

Overall Software Spend

Total annual software spend, inclusive of maintenance, helps define the level of investment necessary to implement the required software asset management capability. In addition to considering the SAM platform, size and complexity of the software estate will guide SAM leaders to team and structure considerations. Across the SAM community, the dynamics required for effective SAM operational execution change at logical levels of annual software spend.

Level 1 - Organizations with total software spend under $25million annually tend to have limited focus on SAM as a dedicated discipline, preferring to have IT operations accountable for deploying and tracking compliance. This is a significant risk as the impact of an 'audit finding' does not necessarily align with software spend. Meaning a small to mid-sized software estate can still have dramatic exposure.

Level 2 - Organizations between $25million and $50million on software spend tend to look more carefully at purchasing a dedicated SAM discovery and entitlement management capability but underestimate the SAM manpower necessary to effectively harvest the information and drive the required activity. Instead, they rely on IT operations to assume this role while SAM is viewed as an analyst function.

Level 3 - As firms approach the $100million in total software spend, discussions concerning the investment necessary for a full SAM operation inclusive of the required staff and platform become far more productive. The issue faced by SAM leaders in this range of firms is the debate between a dedicated SAM operation versus assigning SAM functions across IT operational associates.

Level 4 - Organizations with annual spend in excess of $150 million tend to view software as a strategic asset and will typically have more of a predisposition to invest in a dedicated SAM operation.

Primary Software Publishers

The software publishers that dominate your software estate must be carefully considered as each will have 'approved' software discovery platforms. The challenge is the major publishers rarely agree and a platform approved by one will not necessarily satisfy the requirement of others in your estate. It is important to understand why a platform may be approved by one and not others but we do not recommend this be the dominant selection criteria. Awareness is key so you can plan an effective approach if audited by a publisher who will not recognize your discovery platform. As mentioned at the beginning of this section, system generated reports will help round-out your selected platform's capability.

Level of Environment Change

Every technology environment is a living breathing entity, continually experiencing change. It is important to understand the level of change associated with 'business as usual' operations in addition to major transformational activities. This will help point SAM leaders toward the frequency and depth of reporting requirements and emphasize the importance of alignment with ITSM and Project process areas. These dynamics influence platform selection as well as staffing requirements.

Environment Footprint

There are a number of important factors to consider here. Number of global locations, subsidiaries or environments. Percent of environment that is virtual vs. on-premise. Percent in the cloud and pace at which the organization is moving to the cloud. Number of total devices and endpoints. All of these aspects of a corporate environment help identify the robustness of the SAM platform to continually maintain the required coverage.

Discovery Data Requirement

Prior to starting the formal evaluation process or engaging tool providers, it is essential that SAM leaders fully understand the discovery data necessary to satisfy a 3rd party audit as well as internal reporting expectations. Based on the insight gained in the process of developing the SAM Mission and Value Statements, SAM leaders now have the opportunity to evaluate the various SAM offerings for alignment with expected reporting and analysis. This is an essential step for SAM leaders as they will quickly begin to be told by IT operations that existing internal systems are capable of delivering the requested data and there is no need for a new platform.

Do not underestimate the importance of this item and potential resistance from IT operations. We have seen IT tool teams successfully block deployment of a discovery capability only to quickly disappear when an audit is underway and it becomes evident the solution is inadequate. SAM leaders and their operations absorb an unnecessary hit to credibility as they are required to run the auditor's scripts with a high probability of a significant judgement.

With this basic understanding and completed evaluation, SAM leaders are now ready to determine alignment of a SAM platform with their organization's specific needs, requirements and expectations.

SAM Platform Categories

In the software asset management community, no single vendor or technology solution has taken over the market. Perhaps this is because many organizations view SAM or ITAM as an IT function and believe the existing myriad of tools in the IT environment satisfy discovery and inventory management requirements. Perhaps it is because SAM discovery is viewed as a technical activity. Whatever the contributors, the field of SAM platforms, tools and services continue to evolve.

A word of advice; internal IT operations, IT tool teams and InfoSec need to be closely engaged in the selection process. Each group will have their own view of what the best solution will be for their specific area and will, as mentioned earlier, heavily push the concept that their existing capabilities will satisfy SAM's needs. SAM leaders, while engaging these representatives, need to remain focused on the discovery data requirement to satisfy 3rd Party software publisher audits combined with the information necessary to meet expectations of SAMs sponsors and stakeholders. This will serve as grounding for the team and essentially form the criteria by which tool selection is judged.

Built for Purpose vs. ITSM

Over the past 3 years, ITSM platform providers have pushed aggressively and successfully into the software asset management segment. In the opinion of *The SAM Leader Survival Guide*, this has established a conflict between those that run IT operations and those who are software asset management professionals. As an IT service management tool is the backbone of IT operations and is typically integrated with the asset request process, feeds the configuration management database (CMDB) and is the incident and ticket system, SAM activities such as entitlement management and discovery have become viewed as a natural extension. IT service management solutions fail to fully appreciate the perspective necessary for effective software asset management, lacking the depth of information necessary to effectively manage compliance and supply auditors the level of detail necessary to accurately define compliance at the edition or version level. However, firms such as ServiceNow are investing heavily in their SAM module and will continue to close the gap with 'fit for purpose' SAM tools.

Conversely, market leaders in the Software Asset Management tool category such as Flexera, SNOW Software or Aspera, while built on deep SAM insight, require technical support to effectively integrate with IT operational processes. This has the potential to leave the platform isolated and reduce the benefits SAM leaders can realize.

In addition to the technology considerations, an ITSM heritage SAM module when compared with a SAM dedicated platform will influence staff size and skills. If selecting an ITSM platform as the discovery capability, the staff will tend to be made up of SAM analysts reporting into an IT operation function. When SAM leaders select a built for purpose SAM platform, they implement a dedicated team of SAM analysts reporting to a SAM Director or IT Vendor Management organization.

Each approach has value as well as exposure. In the event of an audit, ITSM oriented teams will be challenged to effectively execute leading to potential for higher financial exposure. If the approach is a dedicated SAM platform and associated dedicated organization, SAM operations must produce the agreed operational value as the level of investment (tool, team, process overhead) will come under pressure quickly if perceived value is absent.

Agent vs. Agentless

Assuming you as the SAM leader have been successful in gaining internal support to pursue a built for purpose SAM platform, the next logical decision point with be the SAM communities' current debate between 'Agent-based discovery' vs. 'Agentless discovery'. This is a very significant debate and one a SAM leader needs to address on multiple levels.

Internal Dynamics: If you have had a debate with the IT organization about the value of a SAM platform versus using an ITSM module, SAM leaders need to expect continued challenges as you move forward. IT operational teams are well versed in tactics to delay or stall implementation of a tool they do not wish to own or have the desire to support. SAM leaders need to proceed with caution as you will hear from IT leaders that SAM 'agentless' discovery platforms put an unnecessary load on the network and can cause severe outages or performance impact. However, if SAM has selected an 'agent-based' discovery solution, IT will point out this technology requires the agent to be placed on every asset which is a tremendous amount of overhead when combined with the need to update or install new releases producing an administrative nightmare for IT.

Platform Sales Dynamics: SAM leaders will hear multiple successful case studies and reference accounts on why their technical approach is the best – speed of deployment and rapid discovery across the environment vs. the level of discovery detail and reporting to ensure all assets are actively identified.

Stay focused on the data requirements agreed with sponsors and stakeholders and the dimensions previously discussed regarding specific software estate characteristics. Remain grounded on these facts and come back to them time and time again to validate alignment and the solution meets the expectations.

SAM leaders need to understand if built for purpose SAM platforms were that superior, there would be broad industry adoption. The reality is no SAM tool executes the full required scope, they are difficult to implement and challenging to maintain. In this case we do need to acknowledge the selection of an agent-based SAM platform places significant responsibility on IT operations.

Tactical License Baseline Self-Audit

This is an area of growing interest across the software asset management community. However, SAM leaders as well as IT operations need to proceed with caution. The offer to scan or help optimize a software environment is a common ploy of software publishers to conduct an audit without having to call it an audit. This is also a common 'offer' from friendly resellers who are interested in helping a client be more efficient with their software spend and identify ways in which to optimize or transition to newer, transformative technologies.

We mentioned this earlier under the 'Rules of Engagement' section of SAM Foundational Elements. It is critical that across the IT and peripheral organizations, any offer to scan the environment MUST be passed to the SAM leader to assess the viability of the offer and any potential exposure that can result. This section is designed for SAM leaders who may be evaluating a self-audit capability.

Resellers Software Optimization Scans: Many times, the reseller account team has formed very positive, beneficial relationships across IT, Sourcing and Procurement. They leverage this to promote the benefits a scan of your software environment will produce while at the same time assuring clients the information is not shared with the software publishers they represent. What ensues is a predictable series of recommendations and activities on products to buy, volumes to increase and other areas to consider. In essence it is a sales opportunity with limited optimization or efficiency gained. We will cover the emerging class of SAM managed services in a moment, but resellers have emerging capabilities in this area. However the core business relationship between reseller and software publisher presents a risk.

Software Publishers: This is a very simple recommendation: JUST SAY NO! However, free offers to assess and optimize a client's environment by the software publishers account team remains a major area of risk and exposure for SAM leaders. When unauthorized discovery data is shared, companies are severely compromised and have no real leverage to challenge findings.

Independent SAM Service Firms: There is an emerging category of independent advisory firms who have developed audit-like scanning capabilities to enable firms to 'self-audit' software publishers and document a factual license baseline. These firms typically have staff of former auditors and leverage the same process and scripts a software publishers' auditor would use.

These independent SAM self-audit services tend to be used on a more tactical basis by SAM leaders. We find these SAM self-audit capabilities will be engaged when a SAM team does not have a dedicated discovery capability or when the SAM team wants 3rd party validation of the discovery data being produced by the platform. They can also serve as an excellent opportunity to see the effectiveness of the Audit Response Team (ART) or an upcoming high stakes renewal which benefit from a 3rd party triangulation of discovery data to identify optimization and efficiency targets.

If this is a consideration for SAM operations, take the time to identify which software publishers present the most significant risk and develop a schedule that aligns with renewals or true-up calendars. Effective execution of the self-audit combined with following analysis and implementation of remediation activities will typically require a self-audit to initiate 4-6 months in advance. Of course, as IT operations become more comfortable in executing the self-audit methodology, the timeframe will reduce.

SAM Managed Service

This segment appears to be a high growth area within the SAM community. Perhaps it's because CIOs are questioning the level of investment and process overhead necessary to support SAM operations. Perhaps it is because an external managed service may be more effective at challenging internal teams and driving accountability. Perhaps it's because the organizations providing managed service effectively speak 'business executive' and there is little interpretation necessary from 'SAM-speak'. For whatever reason, those organizations providing managed services have gained momentum.

As SAM leaders, we need to decide is this an opportunity or a threat. Are we essentially facilitating the outsourcing of our function or are we helping raise the professionalism and effectiveness of the SAM discipline? We believe it is a little bit of both and organizations stand the potential to experience great benefit if they carefully define roles and responsibilities between the SAM managed service and internal SAM office. In essence, a careful analysis of what SAM activity and function is best retained versus those best executed as a service.

It is important to recognize that not all SAM managed service offerings are created equal. While the various offerings will share common activities, the level of sophistication and capability will vary significantly. *The SAM Leader Survival Guide* suggests caution when evaluating managed service providers to ensure they truly have the experience and capability to support your unique organization versus a well-designed slide deck.

Below is an overview of the broad categories SAM professionals should explore when considering a SAM managed service.

Big 4 – The highest profile and most comprehensive SAM managed service offerings today are from firms such as KPMG, Deloitte, PwC and EY. They have strong advisory and assessment capabilities to define Policy, Control and Process requirements. As a highly regarded 3rd Party, they may actually have greater influence driving the required change in these areas than a dedicated SAM leader. They combine this with strong insight to the world of software audits as each maintains a very healthy business supporting software publishers execute audits.

The area these firms can be considered average is their actual entitlement management and compliance analysis. We have found they may not offer remediation advice or guidance on optimization actions that can reduce license consumption. They also likely utilize a private label SAM tool developed as an internal system to perform as the SAM platform. This could be viewed as an average part of the solution, however as previously mentioned, it is the opinion of *The SAM Leader Survival Guide* that no SAM platform is 100% accurate. What does separate this segment from the growing crowd of SAM managed service providers is the powerful manner in which they report and present SAM analysis. Expect a hefty price tag which is why we have observed the decision to utilize a Big 4 SAM managed service is typically made by firms with annual software spend in excess of $200m a year combined with significant internal process challenges.

SAM Platform Providers – Firms such as Flexera, SNOW Software and Aspera have all enhanced and expanded their services capability to offer truly capable SAM managed services. While they may not have the polished advisory capability of the Big 4, they do a very good job across the full SAM life cycle. What they may lack in advisory skill they make-up with a stronger technical platform orientation and effective analysis. We believe this capability will continue to grow as they incorporate lessons learned and gain insight into internal dynamics that challenge SAM leaders and their operations. We have found this category of managed service is less costly than a Big 4, but require a strong internal SAM leader and additional staff to support full SAM operations.

The 'Gang' – With Gartner's recent reports promoting the benefits and growth of managed service offerings to meet SAM requirements, there are an amazing number of firms claiming expertise in this area. SAM leaders need to remain careful when evaluating these firms which could be a software reseller, software audit defense operation or any other firm on the periphery of the software asset segment. As mentioned previously, a key contributor to a SAM leaders challenge is the ability to establish credibility and demonstrate business value. You will need to use your own judgment, but *The SAM Leader Survival Guide* is yet to see this category capable of instilling the confidence necessary to lead or drive strategic value. These offerings tend to be more tactical and many times are in essence a means to sell more products or services.

SAM leaders need to keep their eyes open. It is recommended to engage some of these firms from each of the categories in order to develop deep insight into their services. The probability that one of your leaders will ask your opinion is high, especially with Gartner's very public statements in this area. The ability to state the strengths and weaknesses of these offerings based on your unique environment characteristics will be key to shaping opinion of your executives and as the SAM leader, demonstrate you are considering all potential solutions.

Publisher Scripts

There is a surprising number of SAM teams who utilize the free scripts or system generated reports of the specific software publishers in their environment. We have learned that many times the root cause for this approach is the IT operations and IT tool teams claiming they can reproduce the capability of a dedicated tool by using various features that exist in the environment today or a quick download of an 'optimization' tool from the software publishers web site. Extracting knowledge from system generated reporting is an art. Combining this reporting with an accurate input of entitlements and use rights quickly becomes an impossible task typically leaving SAM operations with little useable data or means to effectively report compliance. Beware the 'we already have the capability' statements. SAM leaders need to be at the ready and prepared to point out deficiencies and short comings of these potential recommendations as IT operations and IT service management teams can be very convincing. Falling prey to this approach can have a dramatic impact on SAM credibility when a 3rd party audit is conducted.

SAM Platform Summary

SAM leaders should explore each of the potential technologies and approaches to develop a SAM operational capability. We recognize SAM leaders are typically under pressure to make a rapid selection and achieve quick implementation, but taking the step to understand all categories will eliminate unnecessary activities and potential dead ends. In fact, as SAM leaders continually report progress to the SAM Exe. SteerCo, confidence grows and the ability to articulate SAM strategy and tactics solidifies.

As we begin the process of engaging platform providers from the above categories, there are several parallel activities that need to be performed in order to have a complete SAM Organization and Operational Design defined to align with platform selection. Several of these become clearer as platform alternatives are eliminated and viable options for your specific environment emerge.

SAM Platform Alignment

With a good handle on SAM platform alternatives, SAM leaders need to make a careful review of internal capabilities and the alignment necessary to ensure end to end software asset alignment. Which systems will be critical to 'feed' information or align with the selected SAM platform upstream? Which systems will the SAM platform need to integrate and populate with asset details in order to support overall process accuracy downstream? What are the reporting capabilities that can benefit from alignment with the SAM platform?

Before engaging in these discussions, which essentially form the requirements for selection of the SAM platform, SAM leaders need to be fully aware that organizations may not view the SAM platform as necessary, claiming current capabilities can meet SAM needs. We have heard this time and time again, only to observe SAM leaders who don't press and challenge ultimately are exposed to serious risk. Understanding what each tool or capability can and cannot do will facilitate productive conversations and help SAM leaders identify pockets of passive aggressive resistance.

The SAM Leader Survival Guide will cover recommended skills for SAM team members shortly. It is important to note at this point that SAM leaders should consider how they can incorporate an IT operational perspective within their organization. This will support an understanding of IT operations and IT service management while enabling SAM leaders to challenge claims of IT tools or processes.

Upstream Process Alignment

Using the software asset life cycle as a guide, it is important to identify those potential integration points and data feeds involving software acquisition. While there may not be direct platform integration, awareness and participation of SAM operations will help ensure knowledge and visibility to identify potential process gaps. SAM leaders need to identify the internal leaders who own the below functions to define where and how the key information will be provided in order to maintain accurate license consumption metrics.

Request/Approval Platform – what are the platforms used for an associate to request and ultimately secure approval of a software license? SAM operations absolutely need to be a key approver in this workflow to ensure a high degree of reuse or utilization of existing licenses and catch non-compliant requests.

Pre-Defined Software Catalogue – ensures alignment with the approved software packages, versions and editions. SAM leaders need to challenge non-compliant requests. A non-compliant request is defined as those software packages that are not pre-populated in the corporate software catalogue and identified as aligned with 'software strategy'. An exception process needs to be defined requiring executive approval. This provides SAM leaders an opportunity for analysis of non-compliant software and the executives who have granted exceptions.

This is the first mention of the concept on a corporate 'Software Strategy', yet it is an important concept for SAM leaders to continually drive with IT executives. With an approved list of software products for workstations, the needs of end user computing as well as data center and cloud installations, SAM leaders are able to not only monitor compliance but support transformation activities.

Purchase Records – Once again, there may not be a true integration with the SAM platform, but SAM operations need to closely monitor what was requested, approved and ultimately purchased. This means a key element is to review the purchase order to ensure accuracy of the entitlements loaded into the SAM platform and confirmation that the purchase order and actual license type and amount are consistent. Not surprisingly, we continue to find when IT teams have secured approval and are downloading the software, they may make a mistake or interpret version and edition choices in very different manner than the Enterprise Agreement (EA). Catching any discrepancies at this point not only helps maintain compliance but provides coaching opportunities to help associates understand the implications of their actions.

Deployment Records – This area will tend to be a hybrid: SAM operations should be part of ITSM change management and release management sessions to ensure the license that was approved, acquired and is about to be deployed is done so in an optimal manner. SAM operations typically don't have this integrated with the SAM platform, but use the ITSM deployment records to confirm alignment with the intended license consumption.

Once again, SAM diligence in this area provides strong coaching opportunities as well as insightful reporting that draws a laser focus to activities and process breakdowns that produce unbudgeted expense exposure.

Downstream Process Alignment

With well-designed process alignment upstream, the SAM platform becomes a critical knowledge repository due to the depth of software asset data that is collected, stored and updated. SAM leaders are able to leverage this information to provide a tremendous amount of operational insight. However SAM leaders need to be very careful to make certain IT leaders clearly understand the purpose of this data versus other IT inventories.

For example, SAM platforms can bring great value to the Configuration Management Database, but it is NOT a CMDB. The SAM platforms focus is to document the many aspects of software including edition and version. When combined with additional environment characteristics such as number of core or virtual CP, insight to the optimization or efficiency can be assessed. It is not intended to document the Configuration Items (CI) or relationship between assets. We have seen many SAM leaders get dragged into ownership of the CMDB or somehow assume accountability for this core IT operations platform.

Alignment of the SAM platform remains with Hardware Asset Management (HAM) information will support retirement of assets in order to ensure any software licenses are harvested and placed into the software library for future use. In addition, HAM data will benefit from SAM reporting 'failed pings' as assets are taken off line but may not as yet be identified or recorded in the HAM platform. This helps facilitate tight control over maintenance cost as cancellations can be issued in a timely fashion.

Reporting Requirements

This is an area where we see the vast majority of SAM leaders underestimate the importance of establishing SAM operations as a team with strategic insight to IT operations. What is meant by 'reporting' is not simply distributing a SAM platform dashboard which tends to be the default communications from SAM leaders. For SAM operations to be viewed as a strategic partner and an enabler of operational efficiency in addition to lessening the impact of an audit, SAM leaders need to provide unique and powerful reporting on which critical decisions can be made.

If we go back to the steps described previously on establishing the SAM mission and value statements, understanding the needs of SAM stakeholders and sponsors, the required SAM Rules of Engagement (RoE), the SAM Policies and Controls for proper software asset usage, SAM leaders have created a 'heat map' of the data importance. SAM leaders need to carefully consider the insights they have gained, the potential output from the SAM platform as well as additional data points from upstream and downstream systems that can help fill some gaps and produce actionable intelligence for IT leaders.

Many times, what we observe is IT and procurement leaders provide a monthly or quarterly dashboard produced by SAM analyst of software consumption. While the data is an excellent representation on current compliance, it typically lacks any connection to business strategy. The dashboard quickly becomes of little value and is ignored by the intended audience. The unfortunate outcome is this reinforces SAM as a tactical operation and prevents SAM operations from extracting itself from being buried as a back-office function within IT operations and ascending to a strategic enabler.

When evaluating the reporting capabilities of the various SAM platform providers or managed service offerings, SAM leaders need to understand that a 'dashboard' will have limited impact with executives. Our goal, as SAM professionals, is to map data importance of each sponsor and stakeholder and see how a potential platform can provide the majority of required data points. When combined with the data available to SAM leaders from internal systems, SAM leaders will be able to build compelling reporting and analysis aligned to the needs of those most influential to SAM operations.

SAM Intelligence Heat Map

As you progress through the SAM platform evaluation process, each candidate under consideration is going to work diligently to impress you with the ability to view a dynamic dashboard with up to the second compliance status. While this is of great value to SAM operational teams and you as the SAM leader, it has little real benefit beyond this 'inner circle'. SAM leaders need to consider the additional internal information sources SAM data is to be combined with. The goal being to align analysis with the intelligence required by sponsors and stakeholders. To do so effectively, SAM leaders should maintain a 'SAM Intelligence Heat Map' by sponsor, stakeholder and business area.

The 'SAM Intelligence Heat Map' can be as simple or complex as you desire. SAM leaders compile the specific information each group and leader have indicated relevant. SAM leaders have uncovered this critical data through development of the SAM Mission and SAM Value Statements. Maintaining a simple grid representing each individual and area ensures SAM reporting has the greatest impact. Produced quarterly or semi-annually, the 'SAM Intelligence Heat Map' reinforces that SAM operations are far more than just software savings. Items to consider for this report include the following:

- Number of deployments by area (Source – ITSM)
- Request by area (Source – Purchasing)
- Software Exceptions by area (Source – ITSM)
- Usage by product by area: (Source – IT tool)
  o Software Usage
  o Processor Usage
  o Cloud Usage

- Budget Alignment Year to Date (Source – IT Finance)

- Forecast & Projection – SAM Analysis

- Recommendations for Optimization – SAM Analysis

- Deployment Improvement Recommendations – SAM Analysis

- Renewal Timing and Considerations – (Source – Sourcing)

The selected SAM platform or service should be able to provide a significant portion of these reports, but analysis can be enhanced by combination with important internal information from finance, sourcing, purchasing and IT service management reporting to provide a truly comprehensive view of software consumption and utilization by area. This facilitates individual meetings with segment owners as well as executive roll-up summaries.

A last word of caution on SAM platform reporting: don't become enamored with the dynamic dashboard. View this as the 'nucleus' on which your strategic reporting will wrap-around and leverage for a comprehensive, strategic SAM deliverable.

Organizational Structure

With a firm handle of the requirements for the SAM platform or service, upstream and downstream process alignment, and reporting requirements, SAM leaders are prepared to develop their organization. The information gathered will help identify the type, size and alignment of the SAM team needed to take full advantage of the technology and meet internal expectations. By taking these preliminary actions, SAM leaders can avoid the basic 'What tool should I buy?' statement and confidently structure the team and skills necessary to produce the desired intelligence.

When developing the SAM organizational structure, SAM leaders need to first define whether the operation is going to be dedicated to SAM resources or a group of individuals who have been assigned functional responsibility. This will dictate team size as well as skills necessary to achieve SAM success.

Dedicated Team OR Functional Assignment

As the SAM leader, you may have inherited the CIO's decision on this topic. As a response to an unbudgeted audit impact, CIOs will typically react to the advice provided by their direct reports. Many times, this advice may be from individuals who do not fully appreciate SAM and perhaps underestimate the challenge. At this time, CIOs debate whether they should fund a dedicated team to deliver on the SAM mission OR do they rely on those individuals responsible for deploying software to execute the identified SAM activities?

Regardless of the initial decision, SAM leaders who have executed the actions described so far in Part 1 - Building a Sustainable SAM Operation, can confidently sit with the CIO, sponsors, stakeholders and members of the SAM Exec. SteerCo and state their intended organizational structure. SAM leaders who invest the time and energy to the items outlined in these pages are successful in securing the support necessary to establish a dedicated SAM team. The outcome being for the SAM team to work in close collaboration with IT operation and the IT service management team (ITSM). Educating sponsors and stakeholders on the mission and value SAM will deliver and carefully defining the data requirement of SAM versus a CMDB or ITSM solution help CIOs see the benefit of a dedicated agenda.

However, there are many successful, productive SAM operations with internal resources being assigned functional elements of SAM operations. If this is the case, SAM leaders emphasize education and training while leveraging the SAM Exec. SteerCo and an extended team of operational leaders in a SAM Optimization Council which is described in detail later.

Size & Reporting Alignment

There really is no industry standard 'rule of thumb'. What we can tell you is the standard approach is for new SAM leaders to budget 'a guy and a tool'. This is a certain formula for disaster. Before putting forward the recommended organizational structure, SAM leaders need to consider a number of areas that will help size and shape the SAM team.

Reporting Structure – Will the SAM team report into a Director or Senior Manager role in IT operations? Will the SAM team report into a SAM leader with a direct line to the CIO, CPO or at the minimum, head of IT Infrastructure? Based on the answer to these questions, the SAM team may be comprised of analyst roles primarily focused on interfacing with the SAM platform or SAM professionals to support execution of the SAM life cycle.

Software Spend – This can also be annual spend by software publisher. Based on total software spend and composition of the Top 5 or 10 publishers, SAM leaders need to align skills as licensing and entitlement management nuances vary significantly across the major vendors.

Level of Change – this can be applied to a number of areas. Level of change in software spend mix and change or transformation in the IT environment can influence the skills and size of the SAM team.

Number of Devices/End-Points – an indication of overall size of the environment. In combination with the selected SAM tool, this may require a full-time database analyst in order to maintain effective discovery coverage.

Selected SAM Platform – In combination with the size of the environment, the selected SAM platform may require a full-time technical resource to support. In addition, SAM analyst, while each tool has similarities, it is best to find team members with real hands-on experience of the platform.

Publisher Reporting Requirements – As publishers introduce reporting requirements such as IBM's quarterly ILMT, SAM leaders need to consider any unique reporting requirements and the implications of these requirements.

These are important elements to define in order to identify the size (#) of SAM team members and the alignment of these team members to effectively cover the majority of software spend.

SAM Skills

Software Asset Management is currently a high growth segment within IT and Procurement organizations. We have found that many SAM leaders come from a broad range of operational backgrounds cutting across procurement, IT operations and vendor management. We also find SAM Analysts can come from IT operations, legal or contract management as well as procurement. The requirement being a keen ability to understand entitlement use rights and deployment breakdowns. In essence, the SAM Analyst needs to be able to extract from the SAM platform the necessary knowledge to challenge, guide and coach on an ongoing basis.

The challenge we typically observe is that SAM operations are their own worst enemy. With teams that are highly technical and somewhat introverted, SAM leaders need to balance skills so there are individuals who can converse with others and have an appreciation for the IT and business operations they support. As mentioned above, don't rely on dashboard graphics to do your talking! SAM teams need to have a diversity of perspectives and backgrounds with the SAM leaders' goal to orchestrate these skills for cohesive performance. SAM operations that include strong IT operations insight, license management issues, audit orientation and finance capabilities produce a powerful combination.

A word of caution before leaving this important subject. *The SAM Leader Survival Guide* believes strongly that SAM is not simply an ITIL process. While there is close alignment and integration between SAM and ITIL, SAM professionals look beyond process elements of asset management and understand the implications of use rights, entitlement management and the impact of deployment on compliance. There is a significant trend for CIOs and IT leaders to view SAM as an ITIL discipline. A close evaluation of ITIL v4's view of SAM quickly illustrates shortcomings regarding entitlement management and compliance measurement. The SAM Survival Leader Survival Guide, while we understand the thought behind this trend, has direct experience with the outcome of this approach and believe CIOs and IT Infrastructure leaders will experience continued challenges.

SAM Organizational & Operational Summary

We have covered a great deal in Part 2 – SAM Organization & Operation Design. We can appreciate the desire to 'get going' and engage sponsors and stakeholders across the organization, but as in all sports, developing a comprehensive playbook anticipating the tendencies, dynamics and expectations of all involved parties is key to SAM success and ultimate survival.

We have identified key elements on which to establish the mission and value of your SAM operation. We have identified the core building blocks of the organization including the platform, alignment required across the organization, reporting necessary to continually communicate the value being derived from SAM operations and the skills or personality of the SAM team. With our plans defined, the next critical ingredient is to establish clear expectations concerning timing to fully operationalize your SAM capability.

PART 3 – SAM Operational Execution

The moment executive leadership decided to invest in a SAM function the clock started ticking. As discussed, executives have likely made this decision due to a negative outcome of a recent audit or IT leadership being challenged by the executive team to identify and mitigate audit risk. What this means is SAM leaders are immediately pressured to produce results and achieve operational capability in a compressed time frame.

The first critical item for SAM Leaders to recognize and understand is the severity of their exposure. SAM Leaders need to avoid the 'SAM tool-centric' syndrome and see the full field of play in order to anticipate and deliver while at the same time stabilizing the SAM function. In essence, upon selection of the SAM tool and securing Exec. SteerCo approval of the organization structure, SAM leaders cross into 'The Danger Zone'.

The Danger Zone

The likely scenario you have inherited is the expectation that a comprehensive SAM function will be established. Unfortunately for SAM leaders, this expectation is aligned with the selection of the SAM platform versus the time required to enable the selected SAM platform. *The SAM Leader Survival Guide* has seen time and time again that executives decided to invest in the SAM function as a way to appease the CFO. The primary focus being 'audit defense' and assurance that software publishers who do issue an audit notification will go away quietly in the night.

With the activities and tactics, described previously, fully executed, SAM leaders have likely spent 4-5 months from the time of the executive decision to fund SAM. SAM leaders are now in the initial stages of deploying the selected platform and maybe in the midst of hiring staff. All of this while the executives expect a fully functioning SAM operation based on expectations that were defined at the outset, most likely by individuals with little SAM insight. *The SAM Leader Survival Guide* refers to this period – the time from the internal decision to invest in a SAM function to the point in time the platform is fully deployed, entitlements loaded, compliance calculated and IT operations implementing identified remediation actions – as The Danger Zone. In our opinion, a significant contributor to the inability of SAM operations to achieve strategic stature is poorly managed expectations during this window of time.

In essence, successful completion and exit from The Danger Zone is in fact crossing the bridge from SAM organizational and operational design to fully functioning SAM operations. Moving from concept to effective reporting and monitoring of the software estate combined with establishing audit readiness with the Audit Response Team (ART). The following activities have been developed to assist SAM leaders understand the importance of developing a multi-pronged game plan at this point in time. This game plan then needs to be combined with clear and precise communications to manage sponsor and stakeholder expectations.

Time to Productivity Misalignment

Industry standard best practice is for SAM discovery to consistently achieve and maintain coverage across +90% of the IT environment. Based on the complexity, level of change in your environment and the selected platform, achieving the +90% target can take an extended period of time. We have found it not uncommon for this period to take 9 months or more from the point in time implementation has started. As the 'long poll' to establishing an effective SAM operation, when executives are informed of this window of time they typically push back and demand more rapid execution aligned to the targets that were defined at the outset of the decision to establish SAM. While this is an uninformed expectation, it is also likely the timeline the CIO has communicated to the executive team. Meaning; we as SAM leaders need to recognize this fact and develop a plan to mitigate risk to our embryotic SAM operation.

So how do SAM leaders survive what appears to be an insurmountable challenge and successfully survive The Danger Zone? How do we avoid taking shortcuts that ultimately limit or eliminate many of the desired SAM platform benefits in order to tell executives the platform is live?

The SAM Leader Survival Guide offers several tactics designed for parallel execution to implement alongside with operationalizing the SAM platform or managed service. These items have been developed to produce intelligence regarding SAM exposure, audit readiness and deployment enhancements to identify areas of exposure and reduce risk, the goal being to produce accelerated SAM value while core operations are being established.

Pro-Active Audit Susceptibility Plans

We're asked time and time again for the key criteria or characteristics that indicate high probability of audit. We will speak of the 'Audit Susceptibility Calculator' later, at which time 18-20 different characteristics will be identified that indicate potential risk of a software audit by a specific publisher. There is no single characteristic that will consistently indicate high probability of audit. Instead, it is a combination of items that upon careful evaluation, produces a cumulative risk profile on which SAM leaders can prioritize with confidence those publishers who pose significant audit exposure. When shared with the SAM Exec. SteerCo or IT executives, this simple activity on the part of SAM leaders begins to shine the light on actions that can reduce exposure and highlight the immediate benefit of the decision to fund a SAM capability.

In parallel to SAM platform deployment and initiation of the SAM Organizational & Operational design elements, we strongly recommend SAM leaders use the SAM Susceptibility calculator to prioritize publishers and develop remedies for the factors driving the risk calculation. You will find details of the recommended factors in the 'Audit Readiness - Internal Preparation' portion of Part 4. In essence, at the outset, SAM leaders are establishing measured assessment of risk with proactive mitigation tactics identified.

Interim Compliance Verification

With identification of those publishers that pose the most significant threat, it is important to execute a plan by which SAM leaders can assess compliance and determine remediation requirements in a timely fashion. Parallel to implementation of the SAM platform and the tactics identified during the 'Audit Susceptibility' process, SAM leaders need to go beyond these measures to quantify exposure. One such activity SAM leaders can implement is to execute self-audits on those software publishers that represent the greatest potential risk. During the SAM Platform evaluation process, SAM leaders have identified the platform best aligned to the environment and SAM mission. In addition, SAM leaders have learned a great deal about the other alternative approaches; one of which was execution of one-time compliance scan or self-audits. While the supplier may not have won the ongoing platform work, rapid compliance verification executed during The Danger Zone has tremendous benefit. Executing SAM Compliance Verification or targeted self-audit can typically be accomplished in 3-5 months, producing valuable software publisher intelligence of those vendors identified as high audit susceptibility, in as little as ten weeks. The impact of this activity for an emerging SAM operation and SAM leader has the following powerful benefits:

Rapid Reporting & Analysis of High Exposure Targets

When the SAM platform is finally operational, the volume of data produced will be significant. It will take time for the SAM operational team to condense analysis into usable, actionable intelligence. Firms who offer SAM Compliance Verification or license baseline services are expert at rapid assessment of the specific publisher's software estate. They identify areas of non-compliance, identify actions that have contributed to the non-compliance, and remediation actions to reduce or eliminate the exposure.

We recommend use of this type of service is carefully positioned as a 'bridge' to SAM sponsors and stakeholders. These firms were likely not selected as your SAM platform as they do not emphasize ongoing monitoring, alerts, ongoing entitlement management or dashboard capabilities, but they are excellent at tactical risk reduction as well as verification of your SAM platform if deployed. Basically, they are fantastic at filling tactical gaps as strategic points of SAM operations.

As we are currently in The Danger Zone, it is highly probable these 'bridge' activities are going to produce surprising insights. In many ways, this is an excellent warm-up for initial reporting when your SAM platform is successfully deployed and helps SAM leaders anticipate where to focus when the SAM discovery platform is fully operational.

Data Discovery Practice

In addition to the discovery data and ability to identify non-compliance, the act of having internal IT operations generate the required data to support the self-audit or license baseline study is an excellent opportunity to observe their effectiveness in this task. Many IT operational teams like to talk about how effective they are at deploying and managing software assets, but they struggle to produce the discovery data necessary to support an audit. This provides SAM leaders early insight into the discipline and capability of IT operations and potential implications for the timely implementation of the SAM platform. This dynamic is addressed in more detail in the 'Audit Response Team' section of Part 4. SAM leaders need to make certain to note the ability of their team to produce accurate, complete and timely discovery data as this is valuable insight to audit readiness.

Entitlement Management Practice

An additional benefit SAM leaders will experience by executing self-audits of those software publishers identified as high susceptibility is the requirement to provide the 3rd party all of the Enterprise Agreement, Contract and Ordering documents for the specific publisher. The firm executing the compliance verification will reconcile entitlements with deployments to produce the compliance position. Many times, what will occur is identification of over deployment leading to discussions with IT operations and procurement at which time missing entitlements may be identified.

SAM leaders can note the efficiency by which the firm currently manages software licenses, areas of consistent breakdowns and opportunities for improvement. All of this, again, is occurring in parallel to the implementation of the SAM platform and integration or alignment with other internal process areas, SAM Policies and Controls as previously covered. This produces additional high-value data to report to the SAM Exec. SteerCo and IT executives during The Danger Zone.

Discovery Data Audit Requirements

An additional benefit to conducting self-audits is the firm you have selected for the exercise will approach the engagement as if they are a true 3rd party auditor. As such, they will typically triangulate the data and identify gaps and inconsistencies between data sources as well as key software identifiers such as edition and version.

Doing this exercise during The Danger Zone provides excellent input to the deployment of the selected SAM Platform to ensure the tool is properly configured to produce the required data fields. This also enhances the opportunity to work with ITSM and Configuration Management Database (CMDB) teams to define where in the request and release process these data points are required to be entered by internal associates.

Deployment Breakdowns

Deployment challenges tend to be consistent across the environment regardless of the software publisher researched. Executing an interim compliance verification or self-audit enables SAM leaders to identify these persistent internal control or process challenges while these important process areas are being created or revised. This insight also supports development of incremental activities to continually coach and support deployment teams to understand the complexities of each major publisher and the impact of incorrect assumptions. It takes time and effort to modify habits. As SAM leaders assemble the Audit Response Team (ART) and clarify roles, responsibilities and contribution to effective software asset maintenance, utilize the insight gained through the self-audit exercise to develop training and communications to support this modification.

Control Effectiveness

Not all deployment breakdowns are due to lack of IT operations to understanding of use rights and license requirements. Many times, the challenge will be ineffective controls whether that be multiple, fragmented purchase channels, delays in internal process to purchase, record and update entitlements, poor release to production discipline or lack of harvesting license content from decommissioned systems. While closely aligned with deployment discipline and accuracy, executing self-audits for those software publishers identified as high risk will help pinpoint opportunities to enhance process and alignment with the selected SAM platform while the implementation and requirements are being finalized.

SAM Reporting & Communication

By executing independent 'Compliance Validation' self-audit efforts with the top three to five software publishers in parallel to the implementation and deployment of the SAM platform, SAM leaders are able to go beyond the typical '% environment coverage' reporting and begin to provide IT executives strategic value. When SAM leaders carefully consider the benefits of the above recommendations, The Danger Zone becomes a period in which critical SAM elements are communicated, setting the stage for the fully operational SAM organization.

By implementing the proactive The Danger Zone strategy, SAM leaders communicate to sponsors and stakeholders:

- High risk software publisher compliance status

- Areas of non-compliance and estimated exposure
- Remediation opportunities and tactics
- Process and deployment gaps which have led to the non-compliance

Can you see the dramatic difference between reporting the above insight versus simply updating the SAM Exec. SteerCo of the percent being discovered by the new SAM platform? There is immediate real value that eliminates the perceived time lag between the decision to implement a SAM operation and receiving actual benefit.

SAM leaders need to seriously consider utilizing a 3rd party to verify software publisher compliance by executing self-audits as a tactic within their overall SAM strategy. Many of these firms who provide these services are run by former auditors who have a very different way of interpreting discovery data and contract assumptions. When utilized for specific, high audit risk software publishers, these 3rd parties bring great benefit as SAM operational teams learn how an auditor interprets the data they look at every day. We talk more about this in the Audit Readiness section but wanted to impress upon SAM leaders that 3rd party independent compliance scans and license baselines are viable augmentation tactics no matter the maturity of your SAM operation.

Publisher Sequencing & Prioritization

Many of the leading advisory firms do a very good job helping SAM teams understand that it takes time to 'load' entitlements and reconcile use rights against discovery data. The assumption typically is two software publishers fully loaded into the SAM platform every month. Meaning that it could take up to three months AFTER the SAM platform has finally achieved the necessary environment coverage before the Top 5 publishers are effectively being reported. This extends the total time from the decision to implement a SAM function to achieving SAM operational value to potentially a full year based on the SAM tool selection and size of the environment. This fact intensifies the pressure on SAM leaders to produce some level of reporting to demonstrate progress. The unfortunate consequence of which is SAM operations report initial findings to satisfy executive sponsors before the platform is stable. This immediately undermines SAM credibility as the initial launch of the SAM platform produces wild swings in reporting of non-compliance.

To ease this predictable challenge, it is strongly recommended SAM leaders execute 3rd party compliance verification license baselines or self-audits previously described. This enables SAM leaders to report results of the SAM platform against a solid baseline while describing for the SAM Exec. SteerCo activities to stabilize the SAM platform that will reduce the variance between the 3rd party license position and initial discovery being reported by the new SAM platform. By doing so, SAM leaders can more effectively guide sponsors and stakeholders through this stressful portion of The Danger Zone.

In order to prioritize software publisher sequencing for SAM platform implementation, we recommend the following data points be utilized to determine the final recommended rollout.

- Software Publisher Audit Susceptibility Calculation

- Software Publisher Total Annual Spend

- Technology Roadmap Alignment of the Software Publisher

- Renewal Schedule

- True-up Schedule

Once developed, SAM Leaders need to educate the SAM Exec. SteerCo on the rationale behind the sequencing of loading software publisher entitlements and reinforce the time to productivity.

Utilizing the SAM Exec. SteerCo

With the right members, the SAM Exec SteerCo provides tremendous benefit to SAM leaders and their ability to establish SAM operations as strategic contributors. This group is not intended to be in name only or a group engaged for formal sign-off. The benefit of this important group is the ability of the members to represent SAM operations accurately when they are in other meetings or engaged with their teams. Realizing the Exec. SteerCo is SAM operations single most effective communications channel, SAM leaders need to carefully consider the information shared and guidance requested during The Danger Zone timeframe.

As SAM leaders work through the process with sponsors and stakeholders to define SAM Mission and Value statements as well as software publisher Rules of Engagement 'RoE", they need to carefully consider which of these individuals has the right political and operational influence to drive support and adoption of SAM requirements. While in The Danger Zone, SAM Leaders need to ensure they are establishing effective group and individual communications with Exec. SteerCo members. *The SAM Leader Survival Guide* recommends continuous reporting against an established baseline with detailed description of the actions or events that have produced the result, whether positive or an impact.

Danger Zone Exit

As defined above, The Danger Zone is the period of time between SAM Platform selection and successful implementation of SAM operations producing stable compliance reporting of a firms Top 5 software publishers. While we have identified multiple items that could have severe impact on the credibility and long-term viability of the SAM operation during this specific vulnerable period, none produces greater exposure than receipt of an audit notification.

Before the SAM platform has been selected, if an audit notification is received, CIOs, CPOs and CFOs will comfort themselves as they have already made the decision to invest in a SAM function. In many ways, this is a positive for SAM leaders as it reinforces the importance of the operation. However, once the SAM platform has been selected and implementation has started, reaction to an audit notification changes dramatically. If an audit notification arrives at this time, SAM leaders are immediately challenged and asked why it is taking so long to become productive? Why are we not ready? How much exposure do we have?

The recommended actions described in The Danger Zone will help reduce the adverse impact significantly for SAM leaders. In fact, if you have executed a 3rd Party Compliance Validation or self-audit for the software publisher that has sent the audit notification, a SAM Leader will enjoy a boost of credibility. Even if it is a different software publisher, the 3rd Party self-audit has helped with identification of deployment, control and entitlement process challenges that can be used to estimate likely exposure of the pending audit.

SAM Backroom Tendency

During the period we have identified as The Danger Zone, an equally important dynamic SAM leaders need to be aware of is the tendency for software asset operations to isolate themselves from IT operations and become 'analysis fixated'. The second critical area of Part 3 - 'SAM Operational Execution' are the tactics necessary to help SAM leaders establish a strategic presence and avoid being viewed as a 'backroom' analysis function that spits out meaningless, non-directional metrics.

SAM leaders need to carefully focus on the tendency of SAM operational team members becoming completely enamored with entitlement data and reconciliation of deployment information to produce the compliance profile. If this becomes the sole focus during The Danger Zone, SAM leaders will never achieve the strategic role intended. As discussed in the previous section, there are a number of effective tactics for SAM leaders to produce valuable insight while SAM operations become fully effective. To do so, SAM Leaders and their team members must be visible and contribute in all areas where software implications occur.

One area where this quickly becomes very apparent is SAM organizations who have not taken the time to develop clear and concise mission and value statements with executive sponsors. *The SAM Leader Survival Guide* continues to see SAM operations attempt to promote KPI's such as 'cost avoidance' due to the effectiveness of deinstalling software as the primary measure of SAM success. Yes, this is an important element of the SAM life cycle, but in many ways, it points to the tactical aspect of SAM, reinforcing the perception SAM leaders have limited influence or benefit to contribute. Utilizing the steps outlined in the previous section on The Danger Zone and other reporting and communications recommendations throughout this book, SAM leaders will be in a far better position to deliver value and ensure sponsors and stakeholders fully appreciate the SAM charter.

SAM Cross-Operational Visibility

The SAM Leader Survival Guide speaks of the importance of integrating and aligning the SAM platform with multiple upstream and downstream processes. This is an essential element to ensure all aspects of the full software lifecycle is viewable, however SAM professionals need to be engaged PRIOR to an item being viewable in a tool. If SAM professionals are learning of an addition or change when it is registered, this represents a potential missed opportunity to provide valuable guidance on software issues at the point a decision is being made. It is also an indication that SAM team members are not present at critical parts of an important process.

SAM operations need to avoid observing the outcome of software decisions and get in the game. Participate in the processes and forums in which software implications can be voiced BEFORE a decision is made to support optimization and efficiency or at the minimum, help a team fully understand the software consumption and budget implications of their decision. Fortunately for SAM leaders, there are a few natural areas to focus on in order to help IT operations improve deployment and environment maintenance disciplines. All IT transformations or changes, no matter the size, follow a predictable process from concept to release into production. SAM Leaders need to carefully look at the stages for each of these processes to determine when injecting SAM perspectives can produce the greatest benefit.

In Part 4, — Audit Ready SAM Operations, we will discuss the importance of forming the SAM Optimization Council which is designed to form linkage between the SAM Exec. SteerCo and operational execution. During the recommended meeting and communications with this council, SAM leaders can highlight the importance of SAM to participate in the identified process meetings and communication workflows.

IT Project & Transformation Process Visibility

Activity in an IT organization can be broadly categorized into two areas: Business as Usual (BAU), commonly referred to as 'Run the Business' (RTB) or 'Change the Business' (CTB) activities. Ultimately the goal of every CIO is to optimize BAU activities in order to increase the level of investment that can be put into projects to transform capabilities. To support effective execution, most IT organizations will have a dedicated, professional project management organization (PMO) comprised of project management experts with strong working knowledge of the IT environment. This team of PM's works directly with the business analysts (BA) or business relationship managers (BRM) who interface directly with assigned business functions within their organization to document business requirements for upcoming projects of all sizes and shapes.

This team of individuals, working closely with business functional representatives, maintain a list of identified projects that will be submitted for a review and approval process – typically a 'Gate' – in which a group of cross-functional business executives agree to prioritization of those programs that hold the greatest promise for the organization. Once approved, these projects are assigned and the team works diligently to move from a high-level estimate (+/- 50%) to produce a more detailed, intermediate project scope in which the cross-functional business executives can give a go/no-go decision based on more detailed scope and more accurate budget forecast (+/- 20%). With '2nd Gate' approval, the team moves into full scale execution, providing status to the executives and seeking approval for additional budget requests. Typically, the last major 'Gate' is approval to release to production.

While an organizations PMO process may be more detailed than the above description, SAM leaders need to recognize that each of the PMO Gates presents an opportunity to review environment, architecture and software implications while enabling the SAM team to more effectively plan license requirements. *The SAM Leader Survival Guide* offers the following guidance for SAM Leaders to reduce surprises and align license requests with deployment impact.

Prior to the outset of initial project scoping and sizing, SAM leaders need to provide input to the estimation template to make certain initial estimated cost and ongoing maintenance cost are considered in the total price. This helps the BAs and BRMs as well as the IT PMO contact understand software implications of their target architecture.

The completed estimate will be included in the business case for review during the 1st Gate of the project management process. A SAM professional then needs to participate in all subsequent gate or formal review sessions. The purpose being to ensure cost estimates remain accurate and identify any potential changes to the software consumption profile for the project and potential budget implications.

If you consider 30-40% of an annual IT budget is aligned to 'Change the Business' activities, significant errors in anticipated software usage can occur long before the solution is deployed into production. SAM professionals have the opportunity to bring value and eliminate surprises while optimizing software utilization. In addition, by being a member of the PMO gate process, SAM professionals are now able to better anticipate the events tracked by core ITSM process areas of change management, configuration management and release management. SAM is also better positioned to assess the impact to ongoing support requirements and help IT finance maintain accuracy on this important budget item.

Being a consistent member participating in these meetings is a significant tactic to create broad visibility of SAM as a function and the value to be realized by more accurate estimates and final project costing.

Enhancement/Small Development Efforts

Separate from the larger Project Management Office (PMO) and formal cross-functional business executive approval process, there are a series of small projects or enhancements that occur in every IT environment. Some of these activities will be for stability or increased base functionality, but don't be fooled by the level of budget as breakdowns in this area, over an extended period of time, can have significant impact on a firm's software compliance profile.

In many IT organizations, small project or enhancement management is the responsibility of an IT Vendor Management Organization (VMO), PMO, or can be approved by an IT leader. If these items are managed and executed by IT operations directly, this can develop into a potential area of risk to maintain software compliance. IT operations teams, application teams and Information Security (InfoSec) staff may deploy small incremental changes with little to no documentation or alignment with the required defined process. An increase in Virtual CPU or other small revisions over a period of time can have dramatic impact on compliance. If not formally managed and documented, SAM professionals represent the last line of defense as the SAM platform should be enabled to monitor changes of this type.

As part of SAM's overall reporting and communication strategy, SAM professionals will be able to develop metrics of 'compliant' versus 'non-compliant' changes with a forecast of software impact and likely exposure in event of an audit. It is recommended SAM Leaders carefully evaluate the manner in which they deliver this analysis within their organization.

Once again, this area of enhancement and small project management represents opportunity for SAM leaders and their operations to be visible. Ongoing measurement and education of the potential negative impact of unmanaged enhancements and small projects puts SAM leaders in the position of providing value and insight that supports overall IT budget efficiency. For those SAM operations that report into the IT operations team, this can be an ongoing area of friction. But handled properly with political sensitivity, SAM Leaders will help these IT leaders maintain budget compliance or help identify the activities that are adversely impacting the budget for IT leaders.

IT Environment Management Visibility

In many ways, a strong and effective SAM operation will be perceived as a threat by those individuals responsible for management of the IT environment. However, if this relationship is properly managed, both parties can receive tremendous benefit.

The first item for SAM leaders to consider is the internal reporting structure and leveling of the SAM organization within this structure. As shared previously, *The SAM Leader Survival Guide* recommends the SAM leader be a direct report to the CIO or the leader of IT infrastructure. In this structure, SAM leaders have the required political influence and executive sponsorship to be effective. However, this does not lessen the need to be sensitive of the impact SAM analysis may have on other IT team members. During The Danger Zone, SAM leaders need to build the correct rapport with IT operations. SAM should not be viewed as a subservient role but one that provides benefit to operations in either performance or efficiency. This information is shared in a positive, proactive manner at a point when the IT operations team can take action versus being perceived that SAM is continually putting them in a hot seat in front of leadership.

As described in Part 1 - Building a Sustainable SAM Operation, the individuals we are speaking of in the IT organization are likely key stakeholders. As the SAM leader, you worked with these individuals to develop the SAM Mission and Value statements. During The Danger Zone, we make certain to work with these leaders and their teams to demonstrate their input has been incorporated into SAM operations with effective, targeted reporting.

An important tactic to avoid is the SAM backroom tendency, to having key IT individuals as part of the SAM Optimization Council provides ongoing reporting and communications reinforcing SAM's overall service agenda.

ITSM Process Engagement

Potentially an area of misunderstanding or conflict is the alignment of the SAM operation with the IT Service Management operation. *The SAM Leader Survival Guide* touches on this subject several times as this is a significant trend today for ITSM operations to assume responsibility for the SAM function. To be effective, SAM leaders need to be clear on their approach based on this crucial relationship.

SAM Operations Within ITSM: SAM leaders who are a part of the ITSM operation or report into the ITSM leader face a significant challenge. ITSM operations based upon ITIL or ISO standard view SAM as a process. While this is an important part of SAM operations, it is the ability to extract knowledge of each step in the process to identify challenges and impact to license consumption. SAM leaders need to understand this orientation and use ongoing education to help ITSM leaders see the soft-skills necessary to maintain an effective SAM operation. The goal is to help ITSM leaders and team members understand the intelligence necessary to effectively manage entitlements and apply reconciliation analysis within the overall workflow.

SAM Operations Adjacent/Parallel to ITSM: As a likely stakeholder, the hope would be that you as SAM leader have taken the time to work with ITSM leadership and develop a complimentary alignment. *The SAM Leader Survival Guide* has observed ITSM leaders quickly shift focus and accountability for the Configuration Management Database (CMDB) to SAM operations if SAM leaders are not careful. Make certain during the SAM platform evaluation process the alignment, interaction and feeds between the SAM platform and CMDB are well defined, documented and communicated. SAM leaders can bring valuable asset information to support inventory, but the role of a SAM platform is to define the depth of data necessary to effectively track deployed software on an asset.

It is recommended that SAM leaders ensure ITSM leadership is part of the SAM Exec. SteerCo or the SAM Optimization Council. By doing so, SAM leaders are able to keep these important influences fully aware of SAM activities, analysis and recommendations.

The SAM Leader Survival Guide has identified the above five areas to establish SAM operations and SAM leaders as strategic contributors versus a backroom function. Every organization offers similar opportunities for SAM leaders to be on the offensive and drive visibility, ultimately supporting perceived value.

SAM Strategic Linkage

SAM leaders need to work diligently to establish and maintain crucial relationships which ensure key sponsors, stakeholders and other politically influential individuals have full understanding of SAM current activities and SAM's operational contribution. To achieve this linkage, creation of a SAM Executive Steering Committee (Exec. SteerCo) at the outset of the decision to invest in SAM provides leaders a necessary forum in which to inform key influencers. Formation and effective use of a well-structured Exec. SteerCo protects SAM leaders and their emerging operations not only during The Danger Zone period, but with ongoing operations.

Every organization is different. However there are a few key, highly influential leaders in IT organizations who essentially surround the CIO and have the ability to reinforce the strategic contribution of SAM operations and enable the SAM leader to maintain visibility.

However, *The SAM Leader Survival Guide* offers a word of warning. SAM leaders need to focus on the SAM Exec. SteerCo and make certain the forum produces value for its members. Many times, the SAM Exec. SteerCo quickly becomes an 'in name only' group with no real activity. The last part of this section offers some recommendations for SAM leaders to ensure utilization of this group is productive for all involved.

SAM leaders need to consider the following key functions being represented in the SAM Exec. SteerCo to reinforce strategic linkage necessary for SAM operational success.

IT Finance

Perhaps one of the functions that benefits most from an effective SAM operation, IT finance is a key stakeholder and most likely a critical 'peripheral sponsor' for SAM leaders to nurture a close productive relationship. As discussed in Part 1 – Building a 'Sustainable' SAM Operation, the leader of IT finance was a key focus for SAM Mission and Value Statement development. Through this process, we have identified the key metrics IT finance use to assess budget compliance. SAM leaders need to ensure these measures are incorporated in the base SAM financial reporting on a monthly, quarterly and annual basis, including trending and forecasting.

A strong relationship with IT finance, based on providing insight and spend data that support IT finance accuracy, provides SAM leaders a valuable ally who has the direct ear of the CIO. The leader of IT finance is a key participant in the review of budgets and exploring the implications of investment decisions. A favorable opinion of SAM stands to offer potential influence when investments or reductions are being considered.

InfoSec

In our opinion, a very close second to include in the SAM Exec. SteerCo is the leader of internal Information Security (InfoSec) or Cybersecurity team. While IT finance has the ear of the CEO related to budget, InfoSec also has the CIOs attention concerning vulnerability and environment risk that could disrupt the business and cause severe reputational damage. Once again, this is a key individual the SAM leader has engaged to develop SAM Mission and Value Statements while attempting to uncover what specific information SAM operations can monitor and produce to benefit InfoSec in their execution. Demonstrating value to InfoSec and while establishing strong synergy with SAM operations.

In addition to having the InfoSec leader as part of the SAM Exec. SteerCo, it is recommended that SAM leaders participate in InfoSec meetings. By doing so, the SAM leader continues to see potential opportunities to add value through effective alerts, patch management status or other key data points.

IT Operations & Infrastructure

The SAM Leader Survival Guide has touched upon the delicate nature of the interaction between IT and SAM operations multiple times. SAM leaders have engaged these individuals in development of the SAM Mission and Value Statements, but real care is required to make certain SAM provides value to these individual leaders versus exposing IT process breakdowns that produce license non-compliance and ultimately unbudgeted impacts.

SAM leaders have the opportunity to continually monitor optimization opportunities for recommendations of a more efficient environment. Continual education on deployment best practices combined with asset utilization estimates, such as percent processor utilization, may help IT Infrastructure leaders achieve improved efficiency. IT Operations leaders may benefit from identification of process non-compliance and identification of methods to correct or reinforce the importance of process adherence.

With regard to influence with the CIO, SAM leaders will need to work hard to have IT Infrastructure and Operations leaders achieve a neutral view. Of course, this is a different dynamic if the SAM operation reports into these functions. The concept of the SAM Optimization Council will be introduced shortly as an additional means to drive visibility of the SAM agenda. Between the Exec. SteerCo and this additional team, SAM leaders need to continually focus on maintaining strong, mutually beneficial relationships with key IT infrastructure and operations team members.

Procurement/Sourcing

The SAM Leader Survival Guide recommends the Chief Procurement Officer or head of the IT Sourcing category is included in the SAM Exec SteerCo. Many times, these individuals are highly influential with an organization's Chief Financial Officer (CFO). A positive working relationship with SAM that supports optimized Enterprise Agreement renewals with credible usage and deployment data will enable Sourcing to achieve their goals of spend management and 'save' identification. SAM leaders are in a unique position to help Sourcing achieve these goals.

These leaders can also have some level of influence with the CIO, but the real value for SAM leaders is when a CFO makes a comment to the CIO about the positive feedback of SAM operations from his team. To establish and maintain a positive relationship, SAM leaders and the leader of Sourcing IT category need to ensure clear alignment with roles and responsibilities with free-flowing communications across operational team members. This will help avoid potential tension and enable all parties to focus on their specific activity in a collaborative manner.

Legal

We will spend more time in Part 4 – Audit Ready SAM Operations – on the importance of having internal council a part of the Audit Response Team (ART). In collaboration with Sourcing, SAM leaders want to focus on ensuring contract management, inclusive of all purchase orders or order documents, is properly maintained and accounted for in a central repository.

An additional critical point of collaboration between internal council, Sourcing and SAM is the specific clauses within each software publisher Enterprise Agreement dealing with audit rights and non-disclosure agreements (NDA). Helping internal council understand the implications of the terms will enable them to more effectively negotiate these items.

Maintaining a detailed calendar of renewal dates with appropriate lead time to accomplish required negotiations is a great asset for internal legal teams.

SAM Operational Execution Summary

The Danger Zone is a very real and perilous period of time for SAM leaders. This section has provided detailed, actionable actions SAM leaders can employ to fill the void during this time and to establish critical reporting and analysis that begins the process of identifying risk and developing appropriate mitigation. All while the SAM platform and team are being formed.

In addition, Part 3 of *The SAM Leader Survival Guide* has identified key members for the SAM Exec. SteerCo. SAM leaders will need to consider additional members based on your organization's specific dynamics. Once finalized, and the team formed, SAM leaders need to develop the strategy to engage and effectively inform these individuals.

The nature of what information is reported evolves as SAM operations progress from platform selection, through The Danger Zone and ultimately achievement of ongoing operational performance. Formal meetings typically evolve from quarterly to semi-annual sessions which are supported by regularly scheduled reporting that summarizes key activities, accomplishments and upcoming tasks. Combining formal meetings, well-structured and summarized schedule reporting with one on one meetings enables SAM leaders to create a well-informed, productive SAM Exec. SteerCo.

Part 3 – SAM Operational Execution is an important reference for SAM leaders to utilize on an ongoing basis regardless of the maturity or performance of your SAM function. The techniques described for effective management of The Danger Zone can be applied at any point a SAM leader feels appropriate. Tactics to resist the tendency of SAM operations to become a tactical, backroom function should be continuously monitored combined with proactive management of those key relationships that enable SAM leaders to earn a seat at the table when strategy is being developed.

With SAM operational execution underway with a strong, sustainable foundation, SAM leaders need to turn their attention to establishing a true 'Audit Ready' capability or run the risk of suffering a debilitating impact to SAM credibility when the audit notification arrives. It is essential for SAM leaders to establish the understanding that response to a software publisher audit notification is a shared accountability across key functions within IT, Finance, Legal, Sourcing and SAM. Each having set responsibilities and contributions to effectively manage the audit and achieve a favorable outcome.

Part 4 – Audit Ready SAM Operations

Threat of an audit from a software publisher dominates the perception of a SAM operations effectiveness. As SAM professionals, we understand the value we deliver across the full software asset life cycle and not simply the ability to effectively manage audits. As previously stated, regardless of the ultimate outcome of an audit, it is the receipt of an audit notification that adversely impacts SAM perception if SAM leaders have not taken the proactive measures described previously.

As an introduction to Part 4 – Audit Ready SAM Operations, *The SAM Leader Survival Guide* provides guidance for SAM leaders to establish and maintain audit-ready capability. However, there is one very important caveat; SAM leaders <u>NEVER</u> refer to the activities and tactics we are about to describe as audit response but focus on subtly establishing the understanding SAM is truly a shared responsibility.

In this section, we will first look at the current audit landscape and then move to tactics and actions to build an internal capability to rapidly and effectively respond to an audit notification.

Software Publisher Audit Landscape

There is extensive writing on this subject available to all who care to research the current software publisher audit environment. *The SAM Leader Survival Guide* looks at software audits through the lens of a Software Asset Management leader and the required amount of internal collaboration necessary to successfully support effective management and closure of audits. We know it's not a question of 'if' but 'when' as well as 'how aggressive' the auditor and software publisher will be in pursuing findings or leveraging an identified non-compliance to capture a net new purchase.

What has brought us to this point? Why has audit management developed to be the primary if not exclusive detriment of SAM operation effectiveness? Who's to blame? Who is actually being taken advantage of?

The SAM Leader Survival Guide believes there have been a few developments that have created this current market dynamic. By no means is this intended to be an exhaustive list. However, as SAM Leaders, if we focus on 'root cause', perhaps we can see a balance or both sides of the challenge. This will help us anticipate potential tactics and tendencies when engaged in an audit.

Software Publisher Perspective

Yes, it is an important 'Intellectual Property' subject and one that Software Publishers protect aggressively and rightly so. Software Publishers spend a great deal of time and effort defining use rights, entitlements and requirements which are detailed in Enterprise Agreements only to see these agreed terms ignored or misinterpreted. Is the inability of a client to adhere to contract terms that have been reviewed and agreed to the fault of the software publisher? Is evoking the audit clause that was agreed to akin to saying the software publisher does not trust you? How else would a software publisher be expected to confirm proper deployment and use of their products?

As SAM leaders, we need to acknowledge that organizations are continually pushing the technology envelope to enable agile operations. This has led to software being deployed and used in new, innovative fashions not contemplated in use right definitions. Is it wrong for software publishers to evolve their metrics and use rights in an attempt to keep pace?

Customer Perspective

Enterprise Agreements, Use Rights, Requirements and License Metrics have become so complex it is a direct effort on the part of Software Publishers to take advantage of their customers. These are shady moves that muddy the waters and make it impossible for a customer to effectively know their compliance position. Why is it a legal exposure if the software is installed but not used? Shouldn't a firm only be obligated to pay for what is used?

Audit Dynamics

The SAM Leader Survival Guide believes both parties have legitimate positions. Yes, a client has a fiduciary responsibility to adhere to the contract terms that they have agreed. Yes, software contracts have become difficult to understand and present significant challenges for customers to accurately and consistently monitor compliance. Gone are the days when you purchased a disk and loaded it onto a single workstation or server. Today we are all aggressively looking at hybrid cloud scenarios and highly virtualized environments. Software Publishers have had to evolve the manner in which they contract and charge for their products to keep pace with the manner in which clients consume and utilize these capabilities. While some Software Publishers may be perceived as overly complex, the reality is that change has been necessary.

Perhaps what has not kept pace has been organizational focus on how to effectively manage and monitor compliance to ensure alignment with Enterprise Agreements. Instead of pointing fingers, IT and procurement operations who have been initiating, negotiating and utilizing these agreements perhaps have been slow to embrace the actions necessary to effectively communicate and manage these changes internally. Thankfully, if you are reading *The SAM Leader Survival Guide*, your organization has probably invested in the SAM function and is likely to have achieved the internal support necessary to bring balance to the relationship with your software publishers and fairness to negotiations based on data driven usage.

The Audit 'Cast of Players'

Audit scope definition, the manner in which the audit is executed, outcomes and final settlement negotiations can vary significantly based on the software publisher and the auditor. *The SAM Leader Survival Guide* is based on the belief that while there may be similarities, each audit is unique. Ultimately it is the interpretation and assumptions of the involved parties that drive activities, findings and final outcomes.

Every Audit has a predictable cast of 'Characters':

The Evil Mastermind – Sitting back behind the action is the software publisher who has invoked their contractually agreed right to audit a client's usage of their software in their environment.

The Henchman - The 3rd party auditor or the internal software publisher audit team engaged to carry out the activity required to develop the compliance profile represented in the Preliminary or Final Result reports.

The Victim - The client SAM or IT leaders identified by the software publisher to be the 'auditee' who must facilitate discovery activities and ultimately negotiate the settlement.

The Judge – The client executive – typically the CFO or CIO – who will ultimately look at SAM operations and 'pass judgement' on effectiveness and capability.

SAM Leaders need to carefully consider the capability of the auditor, the software publisher and their internal ability to effectively manage and settle the audit with minimal internal impact and manageable financial exposure. *The SAM Leader Survival Guide* will cover audit readiness and management of an effective audit response shortly. At this point, it is important to consider 'The Characters' and understand the tendencies and tactics of each with an understanding of their motivation.

Auditor Categories

There are several distinct types of organizations providing audit services for software publishers. What originally was the domain of large global audit firms has changed significantly as the revenue stream for publishers has grown more significant. SAM Leaders need to carefully consider the audit firm and the individuals executing audit activity to determine relative capability. Do not assume the auditors assigned to your specific audit are seasoned, experienced resources.

Despite the background or heritage of an auditor, their desired outcome remains the same: to maximize the impact of their findings on behalf of the software publisher and meet internal targets for recovery. This much is true: software audits are a highly profitable endeavor for the software publisher and their assigned auditor as organizations continue to struggle to reconcile deployment with entitlements.

Software Publisher 'Optimization Service' teams

Increasingly, Software Publishers are building their own dedicated internal audit capabilities. Many times, these teams are presented as providing a valuable service to clients with the goal of helping optimize the environment and ensure solutions are deployed in an efficient manner. These internal optimization organizations, and most software publishers have them, can be very effective as they present themselves as part of service delivery or implementation organization and a friendly, non-threatening resource. In fact, a significant percent of audits starts with a client allowing software publishers open access to perform their analysis. In addition to receiving a brief review on potential improvement or optimization targets, there is usually a formal audit notification or an invoice for unlicensed consumption that follows.

We earlier covered the concept of Rules of Engagement (RoE) to be established by SAM Leaders within their organization. A key item or area of focus should be the ramifications and consequence of an employee providing a Software Publisher unauthorized system data. This is an important item for SAM leaders to not only discuss and provide guidance but formally incorporate into SAM Policies. IT Operations, ITSM or whomever is the point of contact for the request to run a 3rd party script for the software publisher representative without proper authorization should suffer the consequences defined in the policy. In the opinion of *The SAM Leader Survival Guide*, the outcome should be termination for cause as these internal breakdowns can cost an organization significant unbudgeted impact that should have been avoided.

Software publisher internal audit teams executing these 'soft-audit' service offerings have been established to produce and maximize profit. The individuals executing the optimization service are measured by results and outcome. It is a business with the ultimate goal of driving audit revenue in addition to incremental, net-new product sales as a means to reduce audit findings.

Software Publisher 'Hard Audit' Teams

In addition to optimization teams or other internal service teams to execute 'soft-audits', many of the major and mid-tier software publishers have invested in dedicated audit organizations to conduct formal audits utilizing the previously agreed audit right defined in the enterprise agreement. Resources who are a part of this organization tend to have are true expertise and deep knowledge of all contract terms and conditions. As with all audit teams, a target revenue capture has been identified and auditors, upon review of owned entitlements, identify likely areas of deployment challenges leading to non-compliance.

SAM leaders need to understand that the potential is high that the software publisher is using the audit event as a means to solidify their position with the firm and leverage a judgement into a net new product sale that aligns with the technology roadmap, securing ongoing engagement.

Third Party Auditors

Conducting software compliance audits is a highly profitable business for the 'Big 4' and a group of focused, mid-tier audit practices. So much so that these global entities have developed substantial Software Asset Management managed service capabilities as they have direct line of sight to the continued failure of organizations to properly manage their software assets. In addition, the managed service offering serves as a potential career path for employees who start in the audit practice and are seeking to stay engaged in the discipline to help organizations achieve more positive results or outcomes. As far as audit capability or quality of resource, SAM leaders need to be aware that much of the time the third-party associate executing your audit is a new hire and this may be their first assignment.

The business model utilized here is fairly predictable for clients. 3rd Party auditor's performance is assessed based upon 'findings' and the ultimate settlement. This means that 3rd party auditors are essentially incentivized to optimize their findings through interpretation and assumptions leading to potentially overstated penalties. The individuals conducting the audit are being measured on performance as well so, in essence, you as the SAM leader need to match this intensely. The best way to do so is based on real data, complete knowledge of deployment rigor and detailed insight to license and use rights. *The SAM Leader Survival Guide* continues to find this category of auditor may not have been provided accurate contract records and basic errors can be made leading to substantial miscalculation in findings.

SaaS Renewal 'Data-centric' Teams

Before we leave the subject of software publisher audit teams, it is important to note for SAM leaders that while audits as an event rarely occur in SaaS scenarios, SAM professionals need to fully understand license metrics and usage to effectively support enterprise agreement renewals. This is an area growing in importance and will be covered in Part 6, Cloud: The Future is Here, but *The SAM Leader Survival Guide* wants to make certain SAM leaders understand renewals with these firms can be every bit as challenging as an audit.

Software Publisher Audit Behavior: Top 4 (MOIS) & The Fab 5

The SAM Leader Survival Guide believes every audit is unique in some manner. With so many parties and personalities involved it is no wonder that an audit can take unpredictable twists and turns before a final settlement is achieved. Fortunately, there are opportunities for SAM leaders to anticipate areas of focus for a specific software publisher. While the sequence of activities will be the same, the largest software publishers do have unique entitlements and license requirements that point to areas an auditor will focus. This also helps SAM leaders anticipate tactics and be at the ready.

The following is not intended to be an exhaustive list of software publishers that can and will audit a SAM leaders' environment. We offer the following insight as the 'Top 4' identified below typically represent better than 50% of a firm's annual software spend. In addition, we have observed a group of second tier publishers referred to as the 'Fab 5' as they are well known for aggressive audits and at times can be extremely difficult.

Microsoft

Most organizations have significant spend with Microsoft. Typically, in an organization top 3 of annual software expenditure, Microsoft offers a unique and interesting audit risk. With a broad range of products and focus to significantly expand Azure, Microsoft has been aggressive in both true formal audits and offering to assess a client's environment for Azure optimization or transformations. Unfortunately for many, as referenced earlier, a client's technology team unknowingly allows this activity to occur only to be followed by an order form for the products identified in use.

Microsoft's annual 'True-Up' and 3-year renewal cycle appears to make Microsoft audits less threatening than the other publishers. However, it is a challenge for SAM leaders as effective measurement of use and optimization must be constant or run the risk of inflated annual True-Ups. Significant swings in unbudgeted license utilization can cause as much reputational damage as an audit while impacting SAM's credibility with IT finance.

An additional observation for Microsoft is the majority of focus tends to be on workstation or desktop products and O365. While this dominates the renewal conversation, *The SAM Leader Survival Guide* has consistently found better than 70% of a firms

Microsoft non-compliance comes from the SQL, Windows and CIS environments. In addition, MSDN, Visual Studio and other developer tools tend to present a significant management challenge due to poor internal discipline on tool use. Microsoft auditors do a good job of keeping the focus away from these big-ticket deltas until a settlement is near, at which time it may be too late to optimize or negotiate the area of greatest financial impact.

Lastly, Microsoft is putting on a big push for Azure. *The SAM Leader Survival Guide* has observed a distinct increase in Microsoft audits with a potential driver to increase use of Azure and waive the non-compliance judgement.

Oracle

Oracle's reputation for aggressive software audits and holding clients accountable is well deserved. Continued product introductions, product acquisitions, bundling and re-bundling on a frequent basis combined with complex license requirements make maintaining compliance with Oracle products not only a challenge, but non-compliance exposure can reach staggering totals. Virtualization rules combined with a complex maze of options and tuning packs only add to the confusion.

Oracle was an early adopter of an in-house audit function. In this manner, Oracle's License Management Services (LMS) - or however they may refer to themselves currently – are expert in interpreting discovery data to optimize findings. Perhaps it was difficult for a 3rd party auditor to effectively apply Oracle's license requirements or perhaps Oracle wanted to realize a higher margin from audit revenue, but the LMS team is aggressive. Like Microsoft, there is a subset of the LMS team that works with Oracle account teams to offer optimization services. These offers need to be politely declined.

If you are an Oracle client, you may have heard of the term ULA which stands for Unlimited License Agreement. Oracle has had great success with this approach as it maximizes support revenue which is at a +90% margin. The concept of an unlimited agreement also sounds very appealing to CIOs who recognize there is a lack of license deployment discipline and by virtue of unlimited quantity, significantly reduces the threat of audit.

SAM leaders who have established the appropriate platform and monitoring capability should have no fear of a ULA and be ready to support a CIO's decision to renew or 'certify out'. *The SAM Leader Survival Guide* believes unlimited agreements can have great value for an organization. This value is best realized by the addition of continuous and effective discovery analysis of usage and deployment as ultimately this data enables reaching the best decision for your organization.

IBM

The SAM Leader Survival Guide recommends keeping a close eye on IBM at this time. Traditionally IBM has used the services of KPMG, Deloitte and others as the primary means to support audits. However, the recent acquisition of RedHat, who has an aggressive in-house audit capability, may signal a change is on the horizon.

IBM, like all other major software publishers, have a number of enterprise agreement programs to package multiple products in what appears to be an advantageous structure for clients. Complexity is compounded due to the unique combination of legacy applications and leading digital offerings such as Watson and IBM's cloud capabilities.

With IBM, SAM leaders need to be diligent with the contractual requirement to implement, maintain and report quarterly sub-capacity usage based upon the IBM License Metric Tool (ILMT). The reality is the ILMT tool is buggy and requires a great deal of maintenance to ensure the reporting, which is a quarterly contractual obligation, accurately captures IBM environment. SAM leaders tend to believe this is an infrastructure responsibility as it is not the SAM platform. IT Infrastructure teams see it as a SAM activity and one they don't need to focus on. The outcome typically is inaccurate reports leading to dramatic auditor findings which in the end reflect badly on SAM operations. SAM leaders need to consider this likely outcome and take full ownership of ILMT management and report generation. Executed properly, ILMT can help identify an area of non-compliance before the final quarterly report is stored.

The SAM Leader Survival Guide has found IBM's 3rd party auditors can be basing their assumptions and conclusions on inaccurate information or an incorrect interpretation. This is an opportunity for SAM leaders to challenge and push the auditor to defend their findings and ultimately eliminate license deltas.

SAP

In many respects, it was the high-profile legal battles between SAP and a few of their large, global customers that brought visibility to the issue of software audits and the difference in how customers and software publishers interpret use rights. The issues of 'indirect use' and the interpretation of availability, created a tremendous amount of industry discussion of potential risk lurking in every global organizations software estate.

SAP may be the most complex audit exposure due to the number of products, critical applications supported and how truly entwined in the business they are. This is why organizations faced with the daunting challenge of transforming to S/4HANA are so concerned. To make this migration without business disruption and minimizing audit exposure will test IT and SAM operations alike.

The SAM Leader Survival Guide believes the level of SAP audit activity will increase as clients consider alternatives to S/4HANA or exhibit hesitancy to upgrading.

Salesforce.com

Before we leave this section on the primary software publishers who dominate audit activity, we need to call out salesforce.com as a 'game changer'. While not an audit, salesforce.com has established a renewal dynamic that is every bit as challenging for SAM operations and IT organizations as they are masterful at data analysis. This analysis is used to drive renewals and associated pricing, leading to substantial increases in spend that may potentially be based on non-optimized metrics. SAM leaders and SAM professionals need to gear-up for this new, high-stakes game with their leading SaaS partners.

The Fab 5: MicroFocus, Quest, Corel, Adobe, RedHat

As stated previously, this section is not intended to be an all-inclusive, exhaustive list of software publishers who audit their customers. *The SAM Leader Survival Guide* has observed the firms identified in 'The Fab 5' as software publishers who are active and aggressive in auditing their client base. While each may have their own reasoning, the common thread is the large number of products offered by these firms, multiple licensing models and the manner in which these products are deployed.

SAM leaders need to be on guard with these vendors. While the outcome tends to be significantly less exposure than the large software publishers, it may well have a negative budget impact and a negative impact to SAM reputation. Because we have not mentioned firms such as VMware or Citrix, we do not mean to indicate these are any less a potential audit risk than others. We have just seen greater activity and more aggressive behavior from those categorized as 'The Fab 5'. Shortly the concepts of assessing audit readiness and audit susceptibility will help SAM leaders implement a more scientific determination of audit likelihood.

Software Publisher Landscape Summary

Before engaging the broader internal team, who will be called upon to form the essential 'Audit Response Team' (ART), SAM leaders need to carefully consider each of the above aspects and dynamics of a software audit. It is recommended that SAM leaders develop high-level, publisher specific audit game plans identifying tendencies and potential areas of exposure within your IT environment. This is best accomplished as a private SAM exercise, the goal being that SAM leaders create a draft plan prior to engaging the broader audience, whether it be the SAM Exec. SteerCo or SAM Optimization Council.

Audit Readiness - Internal Preparation

Before we begin to dig into the tactics and activities to establish an audit ready operation, it is important to fully understand the mindset necessary for SAM leaders to succeed. An 'Audit Ready' SAM MEANS the organization is prepared BEFORE an audit notification is received. It means the analysis produced by SAM operations ANTICIPATES areas auditors will focus on when conducting their audit. It means SAM leaders have established ONGOING COMMUNICATIONS in the form of reporting and effective analysis that calms internal anxiety and allows SAM leaders to execute the full SAM agenda.

The SAM Leader Survival Guide prescribes three core activities that will enable SAM leaders to achieve audit readiness and maintain calm in the face of an audit. The areas are remediation of compliance areas auditors will focus, formation of an ongoing advisory team and preparing an Audit Response Team (ART) for coordinated and effective performance.

Auditor Mindset

We have discussed the importance of selecting a SAM platform or managed service based upon the specific requirements of your organization. It is the opinion of *The SAM Leader Survival Guide* that a SAM platform will produce perhaps 80% of the data necessary for an audit. In addition to tool limitations, the typical SAM analyst simply does not think like an auditor. SAM analysts become consumed with their reporting dashboard and may not understand or anticipate the missing data an auditor will use to drive findings. This is why it is recommended to have a 3rd party conduct license baseline self-audits as this helps identify SAM platform information gaps while showing SAM team members the mindset necessary to challenge an auditor.

The combination of system generated reports with core information produced by your SAM platform will help SAM teams perform the important task of data triangulation and anticipate auditor tendencies and areas of focus. By doing so, SAM leaders can continually monitor and report improvement in these targeted areas building confidence of audit readiness across the organization.

Software Edition

This may seem obvious, however there is typically a substantial gap or misunderstanding about what a firm owns and what is deployed. This occurs in both the workstation side of the environment as well as in server operations. Procurement has purchased standard edition licenses yet individuals download a higher edition such as enterprise or data center licenses. This breakdown can occur at multiple steps in the deployment process; however, the impact is the same: essentially the standard edition licenses become 'shelfware' and the installed software is non-compliant producing substantial audit exposure.

Most SAM operations do not effectively track this critical piece of data point as their platform records software name but may lack edition or version information. In the event of a live audit, this is the exact data the software publisher will utilize to determine compliance. *The SAM Leader Survival Guide* recommends SAM leaders continue to look at methods to validate and augment the SAM platform if it is not capable of measuring and tracking software edition and version with the use of system generated reports and other targeted tools such as Microsoft's Application Panning toolkit (MAP).

Reporting this level of analysis to the SAM Optimization Council, that will be discussed shortly, creates excellent awareness across IT, Finance and Procurement organizations on the criticality of aligning edition and version implementation with license entitlement. Carefully educating the council on the major programs such as Oracle, IBM, Microsoft and others in the environment of what is owned, what is being deployed and any identified gaps.

Metric Implications: Usage vs Installed

An additional deployment challenge observed by *The SAM Leader Survival Guide* has to do with a clear understanding of a software license consumption metric: usage versus installed. This becomes a very significant challenge as software products can mistakenly be added to a server or workstation standard image by IT teams under the impression the software will only be licensable if it's used.

SAM leaders need to ensure they are educating the SAM Optimization Council and all those who deploy and harvest assets on the various license metrics per software package and the importance of managing 'image-sprawl'. In the event of an audit, if the software is discoverable, SAM leaders will have challenging negotiations if their only defense is non-use. This may not be much of a focus for IT teams as many are under the impression if the software is not being used, then there is no cost. This is a troubling and challenging yet very real issue SAM leaders need to address.

Carefully utilize use data to identify software assets that are sitting cold. Identification and removal from the environment will reduce any last second clean-up scramble when an audit notification arrives, enabling the team to focus on a proper response.

Core Optimization

As license measurement has moved from system count to processor count to core and socket count, it has become a very real challenge for IT infrastructure teams to maintain an accurate understanding of each products core minimum. The outcome is license consumption becomes inflated as deployment teams may have two licenses assigned when the product deployed has a 16-core minimum. This grossly drives license count with little to no productivity.

SAM leaders need to create a basic table of 'minimum core

requirements' by product to help IT infrastructure teams optimize clustering and server density to achieve an efficient environment with optimized license consumption. As part of ongoing discovery, analysis and use of system generated reporting, SAM leaders need to help IT teams better optimize clustering and server density for more efficient software consumption.

Virtualization

It is impossible to talk of core optimization without understanding the challenge of maintaining appropriate virtualization and clustering of licenses. Of course, the most visible and publicized issue in this category is Oracle's position with VMware. However, Oracle is not alone in the focus on effective clustering or management at a sub-capacity metric.

Utilizing the data output from the SAM platform, SAM leaders have the opportunity to report core per cluster. Utilizing the knowledge of minimum's and deployment requirements, SAM leaders need to use the SAM Optimization Council to document how virtualization drives license consumption and the specific applicable rules by software publisher.

Anticipating the areas of an auditor's focus, and continually reporting improvements in these targeted areas producing a high degree of compliance, helps SAM leaders build the confidence of stakeholders and sponsors.

SAM Optimization Council

The SAM Leader Survival Guide suggests SAM leaders utilize the team who ultimately forms the nucleus of the Audit Response Team as an ongoing, operational 'SAM Optimization Council'. Perhaps quarterly or semi-annual formal sessions should be held in which the SAM leader provides members of this council detailed briefings on software spend, deployment opportunities, process observations and improvement recommendations. In this manner, SAM leaders establish an important line of communication and dialogue while reinforcing the involvement of these individuals to support effective management of software assets. When aligned with the SAM Exec. SteerCo, SAM Optimization Council members form important linkage between executive and IT operations. This enables SAM leaders to continually reinforce SAM execution while delivering analysis to those who own key process areas.

The moment an audit notification is received, the SAM Optimization Council's focus shifts and members become the Audit Response Team.

SAM Optimization Council / ART: **Stakeholder Identification**
We will shortly suggest an Audit Response Team agenda to utilize which will help identify the skills necessary for a complete ART and those to be targeted for the SAM Optimization Council. Many times, when an audit notification is received, executives and SAM leaders look to severely limit the individuals who have knowledge of the audit and attempt to suppress any communication. This is damaging in several ways as it creates the very real impression that SAM owns all aspects and are accountable for the outcome, relieving any other teams' responsibility to help or take effective actions to remediate exposure. Establishing the SAM Optimization Council eliminates this unhealthy SAM dynamic and allows SAM leaders to orchestrate audit response activity.

The SAM Leader Survival Guide offers the following guidance to SAM leaders as they identify those individuals who can support audit response activities while at the same time serve as excellent influencers trumpeting the benefits of SAM operations as members of the SAM Optimization Council.

Aim at influential 'operational influences': Many times, SAM leaders want to engage executive or senior management participants as members. These individuals, while important, will not cascade communications regarding SAM operations and many times are ineffective at mobilizing the support necessary for an audit response. Don't aim too high or low. Find that middle ground -- people who report into leadership and still have operational accountability.

The areas SAM leaders need to target for participation in the SAM Optimization Council include IT Finance, InfoSec, Sourcing/Procurement, IT Infrastructure, IT Application/Development, Legal, IT PMO and IT operations. There may be additional areas or functions within your organization to consider, but this represents a comprehensive approach for the SAM Optimization Council.

SAM Optimization Council / ART: **Roles & Responsibilities**

As SAM leaders look to establish the SAM Optimization Council, they will need to articulate the purpose and goal of this team and the expectations of members. Maintain alignment with the SAM mission and value statements that have been developed based upon input from sponsors and stakeholders. Define how the SAM Optimization Council will be utilized to gather input from its members to support refinement of SAM strategy and execution tactics and bring benefit to each of the individual areas represented in the council. As members of this group represent the key parties who influence the request, deployment, management and ultimately harvest of software asset, the SAM Optimization Council has a hands-on, operational level view that brings valued insight to challenges and opportunities for SAM improvement.

Formation of this team enables SAM leaders to solicit input from a valued cross-functional team while also creating a targeted team to be 'in the know' when an audit notification is received. In this manner, SAM leaders utilize the natural desire of individuals to be a part of a select group and to be included in confidential information. It is this dynamic that allows SAM leaders to utilize the SAM Optimization Council as the Audit Response Team when the time comes.

SAM Optimization Council / ART: **Inputs & Contributions**

SAM leaders will quickly identify that many of the items recommended for discussion with the SAM Optimization Council are the exact items an Audit Response Team would address under the pressure of a live audit. By addressing these items in advance, SAM leaders are able to fully inform council members what the item is, the importance, how it's used, potential impact during an audit and potential negotiation or challenge strategies. SAM leaders, through their use of the SAM Optimization Council, in addition to informing members, are in fact preparing these individuals for an audit response, avoiding the typical 'audit scramble'.

SAM Optimization Council / ART: **Core SAM Templates**

There are a number of important, basic templates SAM leaders can create to educate members of the SAM Optimization Council and solicit input and recommendations to improve alignment with council member needs. Many times, the information incorporated into the simple templates have limited distribution, but familiarity and review with council members supports effective team response when a formal audit is underway.

Audit Clause Summary

We spend all this time concerned that an audit notification will arrive but rarely take the time to fully understand the exact rights, timing and requirements for a specific publisher. The actual audit notification letter will likely state a timeframe that may not be aligned with the terms in the Enterprise Agreement or accurately state the intended scope of the audit. This immediately throws an organization into panic leading to counterproductive activity.

SAM leaders should create a simple excel file that summarizes the exact audit language for each major (Top 10) software publisher by spend or business importance. Sharing this table with members of the SAM Optimization Council, discussing the implications of the language and soliciting recommended revisions establishes a common understanding across council members. Key items to detail include complete audit clause language, response time and a 'recommended initial response' if an audit notification is received from that publisher.

Non-Disclosure Agreement Summary

Closely aligned to the audit clause summary by major software publisher, it is equally important to discuss with the SAM Optimization Council the appropriateness of the Non-Disclosure Agreement (NDA) in each software publishers Enterprise Agreement. The goal for SAM leaders is to present a consolidated view of agreed NDA language, review if it appears to be sufficient, and when an audit notification arrives, anticipate what will be the appropriate response.

SAM leaders should propose two separate approaches to the SAM Optimization Council concerning an effective NDA. First, if the audit is being executed by a 3rd party audit firm, SAM leaders work with legal and the SAM Optimization Council on development of a '3-way or trilateral NDA'. This is important to establish the necessary protection and use of your organizations discovery data when being shared by the 3rd party auditor with the software publisher that has hired them to conduct the audit. Many times, the scripts and discovery data submitted to a 3rd party auditor may contain information beyond the intended scope of the audit. This information can provide the software publisher insight to your environment that ultimately compromises an organization. SAM leaders want to make certain to limit the ability of a software publisher to see more than data required to satisfy the audit and that the information is used for this single purpose after which it is properly destroyed.

The second audit NDA scenario will be executed by a software publishers internal audit organization. In this case, SAM leaders should ensure the NDA is specific about scope, sole purpose of the information being provided and distribution limited to the requesting party.

Stepping through these discussions prepares the team with a solid understanding of the initial action that will be taken when an audit notification arrives.

Auditor Script Sign-off – InfoSec Process Definition

Discovery data reconciled against license entitlements forms the basis of any audit. Auditors must secure the necessary data and asset detail in order to effectively determine non-compliance deltas. Rarely do SAM platforms provide all of the insight and context necessary, leading auditors to request system generated reports and potentially running specific auditor scripts. SAM leaders, utilizing the SAM Optimization Council, have the opportunity to pre-define the process by which a 3rd party script will be approved by Info-Sec, establishing key expectations such as liability for any adverse system impact.

Having this process defined in advance again helps the SAM Optimization Council see the full range of issues and importance for close coordination of an audit from the outset. It is an additional tactic for SAM leaders to control the pace of audit proceedings allowing time to remediate any potential known areas of non-compliance.

SAM Policy Review

The final area for SAM Core template review is to engage the members of the SAM Optimization Council to provide input in the SAM Policy statements. On the heels of discussing the previous legal elements of every audit, SAM leaders can tie the importance of policy adherence to effective maintenance of compliance. As previously outlined in *The SAM Leader Survival Guide*, a combination of Software Usage Policy Statements is rapidly becoming a requirement for effective accountability. This team is in an excellent position to comment and help drive adoption of these policies.

Taking these actions enables SAM leaders to develop an engaged team that contributes key inputs to the initial activities necessary to determine the appropriate response to an audit notification. Next, SAM leaders need to turn the attention of the SAM Optimization Council to those core processes necessary to maintain appropriate controls.

SAM Optimization Council / ART: **Process Alignment**

In many respects, an auditor draft effective license position (ELP) or preliminary findings are a reflection of an organizations internal process breakdown. Somehow a well-intending associate deployed something in a manner which triggered unanticipated license consumption. This is an excellent area for SAM leaders to focus members of the SAM Optimization Council on as this will enhance audit readiness as well as raise awareness of the need for process adherence.

Having this as a core part of the council's goals and objectives also helps individuals who may question why they are being asked to join. SAM leaders should use the software asset lifecycle to help shape the areas of focus in addition to making certain each process area is represented in the council.

Contract Management

Not surprisingly, effective Contract Management is a cornerstone of any effective SAM operation. As the SAM Optimization Council has representatives from multiple operations, their perspective will help identify areas that may be out of bounds such as independent business units or global offices that may be utilizing other agreements.

Maintenance of a central repository of all Enterprise Agreements and order documents to continually maintain an accurate count of license owned is a natural point of collaboration for SAM leaders leveraging their SAM platform to support legal, sourcing, purchasing and IT finance. The SAM Optimization Council is a great opportunity to continually identify improvement opportunities.

Procurement/Purchasing

Following closely on the heels of contract management and impacts the ability of SAM operations to maintain the required compliance diligence is process alignment with Sourcing and Purchasing. While IT service management is the platform where all IT requests are to be logged and recorded with sufficient detail, it is the predefined approval of workflow integration with the procurement platform which ensures purchases are appropriately recorded. SAM representatives are not only made aware of the request but are able to provide guidance on license availability and reuse prior to approval.

The SAM Optimization Council is an excellent place for SAM leaders to report compliance and identify process improvement opportunities that lead to improved accuracy of entitlement management.

Deployment Controls

The next core process for the SAM Optimization Council to continually review is alignment between what is requested and approved, what ultimately is downloaded, how it is deployed and the environment on which it is deployed. This may be the hardest area to automate. To be effective, SAM leaders will need to monitor multiple data sources and piece together evidence in an investigative fashion to identify deployment habits producing inefficient license results.

The SAM Leader Survival Guide continually observes this area to be a significant challenge for SAM leaders. The root cause of much of the non-compliance experienced by organizations is the inability to track edition and version. A team may request 'standard', securing the required approvals, and download the 'enterprise' edition. Rules, requirements even of the minimum number of core can have a major multiplying impact to license consumption.

The SAM Optimization Council is an excellent forum to educate on the specific license type owned and begin to report process breakdowns leading to non-compliance. Leveraging data from the SAM platform and other system generated reports, SAM operations can document software edition requested and approved, software edition downloaded and the environment

– virtual or physical – the software was deployed. Identifying this early and using the data to educate the team produces a number of positive outcomes. Council members see firsthand the effectiveness of SAM reporting, are able to communicate to their organizations the need for diligence and the consequence for breakdowns. In addition, The SAM Optimization Council members will be aware of the reporting SAM provides the Exec. SteerCo., in which they will want to ensure proactive remediation is identified before an executive ask for clarification.

IT Finance Reconciliation

Tracking of software spend is a significant challenge for IT finance. Gone are the days where procurement simply handed out keys one at a time. Based on how it is deployed, that single license could multiply exponentially. And with that, so the cost. By participating as a member in the SAM Optimization Council, IT finance observes firsthand the number of areas which impact compliance. This helps SAM leaders significantly. When issues arise regarding unbudgeted impact due to items such as data center transformations where the infrastructure team increased processor 'density' without considering software implications, this would be discussed in the SAM Optimization Council prior to being escalated to the SAM Exec SteerCo.

IT Service Management

The SAM Leader Survival Guide believes the SAM discipline is closely aligned with ITSM and there is mutual benefit to be realized through a close and collaborative work environment. It is the matter of perspective and orientation that ultimately separates the 2 disciplines. Yes, effective software asset management requires consistent process. However it is the level of detail and interpretation of use rights reconciled against deployment analysis that determines liability. ITSM teams typically struggle in this area leading to audit exposure.

Utilizing the SAM platform, SAM leaders have the opportunity to report and track non-compliant changes outside of the defined change management process. In addition, SAM leaders can effectively report patch currency utilizing software publisher notification aligned with change management data.

Ultimately, SAM operations can quickly shed light on an organization's discipline to adhere to defined process whether it be measured against ITIL or ISO based standards.

IT Project Management Office

Having the head of the IT PMO as a member of the SAM Optimization Council forms an important link between current environment and upcoming programs to be introduced into production. It is also important for the SAM leader to participate in PMO formal gate meetings in order to understand software and environment implications. By being present, the SAM leader or key SAM team member can quickly offer guidance on software implications. In addition, the SAM team is now prepared to see when the project is released into production that the architecture and environment are consistent with what was designed.

Before we dig into the opportunity SAM leaders have to report valuable operational intelligence to members of the SAM Optimization Council, it is important to recap the importance of the items identified. We recognize executing the above described activities could quickly consume a disproportionate portion of a SAM leader's day. The detail provided is intended to help SAM leaders consider which of these areas make the most sense to include, based on your organization's unique dynamic. By describing each item in the detail provided, the goal is to help identify who would be best to include in the council and for what reason or benefit to SAM operations.

In summary, there is a two-pronged goal of establishing the SAM Optimization Council: prepare the internal team for effective audit response AND establish the understanding that every organization and team plays an important role in supporting effective software asset management.

*SAM Optimization Council / ART: **Ongoing Reporting & Analysis***

Throughout *The SAM Leader Survival Guide*, effective communications and delivering value through deep, operational intelligence has been a consistent and core message. We have discussed the need for SAM operations to avoid being viewed as a backroom function or simply a group of analysts spitting out dashboards, highlighting software measures that lack linkage to business drivers. The reason behind this continued focus is that SAM leaders typically fail to realize the importance of 'actionable data' versus information overload.

SAM leaders have a tremendous opportunity to utilize the insight gained not only from the SAM platform but all of the process interfaces viewed. Taking the time to examine possible analysis that can come from utilizing these various data points across the landscape enables SAM leaders to deliver unique and insightful analysis.

Every organization is different, however there are several consistent areas where SAM leaders can effectively build powerful, actionable insight to support IT.   As you review the following items, think about how this can best be presented in your environment. SAM tools have good graphics, but should you consider a data presentation capability to produce powerful graphics and analysis? How can you best pull together data from multiple sources to present an integrated view? How much is too much? How often should you provide analysis for each group, including sponsors, stakeholders, Exec SteerCo and SAM Optimization Council?

SAM leaders also need to consider how much information and how quickly to provide this level of analysis. *The SAM Leader Survival Guide* has seen SAM leaders delay reporting because they did not feel it was comprehensive as they waited for the SAM platform to be fully deployed. This produces a gap between operational execution and outward visibility that many times adds to the challenges earlier described in The Danger Zone. Other times, SAM leaders move too quickly and do a 'data-dump' that overloads the target audience and quickly causes data fatigue. It is recommended SAM leaders create phases, starting with basic information and then, over time, adding more sophisticated analysis. In this manner, the individuals are more capable of absorbing the information and see firsthand the evolution and growth of the SAM function.

Keep these in the back of your mind as you consider the following suggested analysis. While this section of *The SAM Leader Survival Guide* primarily is focused on the SAM Optimization Council, think about the other key influencers such as members of the Exec. SteerCo, sponsors and stakeholders as each will have unique communication opportunities.

Software Spend Intelligence

This is an interesting and challenging area for SAM professionals. *The SAM Leader Survival Guide* has worked with dozens of SAM leaders and are continually surprised by how few can quickly state an accurate annual software spend. How can a SAM team be seen as strategic if we don't fully understand the scope managed? How can we be an asset to IT finance, IT leadership and sourcing if we are not able to state definitively total annual spend, trend implications of this spend, the top 5 by spend and emerging software publishers in the environment.

With SAM operations successfully integrated into the previously outlined process areas, SAM leaders will have a strong handle on the activities leading to upcoming purchases (PMO alignment), know what is in the current queue for approval (procurement/ purchasing alignment) and view environment changes that can generate incremental license impact (change, configuration and release management). Combined with continual engagement with sourcing for renewals and entitlement upgrade and downgrade implications, SAM leaders not only need to know software spend dynamics but must establish themselves as the ultimate authority in this basic but critical area.

SAM leaders need to hold a close examination of the following software spend areas as a basic foundation for SAM communications. Leveraging all we have learned through the process of establishing our SAM mission and value statements with sponsors and stakeholders, combined with insight from the SAM Exec. SteerCo and SAM Optimization Council, SAM leaders should be able to identify the key spend data points of value to each of these teams and individuals.

Total Annual Software Spend - SAM professionals should always have a firm handle on total annual software spend inclusive of maintenance and support. In addition, SAM leaders need to be able to quote forecast and the dynamics leading to an increase or decrease.

Spend by Publisher – Detailed insight to current spend and emerging trends for the leading software publishers in your estate is an additional level of detail SAM leaders need to document and report with the benefit of analysis.

Spend by Business Unit – Software spend by business unit requires a bit more effort for SAM leaders to understand. Many times, this may be more of an analysis of projects in the pipeline by business unit, but the analysis can be combined with a profile of what software is being utilized compared with other units. Potentially it can be a discussion on application or product rationalization.

Spend by Application – A great area of benefit is for SAM to develop a view of spend by application. Combined with potential upgrade or end of life analysis, SAM leaders can deliver powerful insight to spend and potential upcoming events that may require incremental funding.

The SAM Leader Survival Guide offers the above examples to help stimulate ideas relevant to your organization and specific situation. Also, it is recommended SAM leaders consider the various teams (Exec. SteerCo, SAM Optimization Council,

Sponsors, Stakeholders) and evaluate what level of reporting appropriate for each. Be careful not to try to do too much too quickly. Build a schedule by which you will expand the level of analysis, allowing the audience to get comfortable with the analysis versus overwhelming them.

Transformation Monitoring

Previously we covered the importance for SAM leaders to be engaged in project management check points or gate meetings in order to track the consistency of software estimates based on the required environment or platform. For the SAM Optimization Council, SAM leaders need to report effectiveness of these initial estimates tracked through actual deployment. This again enables the team to see not only breakdowns in deployment, but also identify potential improvements in initial project estimation. This is particularly helpful for IT finance as they have the records of the actual software cost for implementation and accurate estimates for support and maintenance.

We have spent a great deal of time outlining recommended agenda and reporting items SAM leaders should consider for the SAM Optimization Council. The goal of this important linkage between IT leadership and IT operations is to establish a team of individuals fully briefed on all aspects of software asset management. To establish effective management of this valued asset is a shared responsibility AND when the time comes, council members are ready to respond to a software publisher audit with clear and understood roles and responsibilities as members of the Audit Response Team (ART).

Audit Response Team (ART) Agenda

Everything leading up to this point has been designed to help SAM leaders prepare the organization for the eventual receipt of an audit notification. Implementation of these concepts and activities places SAM leaders in a position of strength with a predefined team at the ready. Failure to implement these preemptive actions quickly shines a spotlight on SAM leadership when an audit notification is received, negatively impacting credibility of the SAM operation.

So here we are! As SAM leaders we have worked closely with the identified SAM Sponsors and Stakeholders utilizing their input for clear mission and value statements. We have carefully taken the steps to establish strong SAM operations including close evaluation of SAM reporting requirements, and alignment with upstream and downstream processes key to maintaining effective end to end software asset management. We have formed and are effectively reporting SAM optimization opportunities to the SAM Exec. SteerCo. and the SAM Optimization Council. Now, with the receipt of the audit notification, we as SAM leaders are ready to lead and coordinate an effective audit response.

Audit Notification Review

It is important to take the time to fully understand the audit request and its implications. As part of the SAM Optimization Council, SAM leaders have created an Audit Log of the specific audit rights language with each major software publisher. As the ART carefully reviews the statements in the audit notification, SAM leaders ensure alignment with the language from the Enterprise Agreement. Your legal or procurement organization may have negotiated different terms and response period definitions so it is essential to compare these. Many times, auditors utilize form letters and standard versions of agreements that do not reflect the specifics of an individual's unique contract.

Audit Scope Review

Ensure the scope of the audit is clearly defined including affiliates, potential join ventures or majority owned businesses as well as the technology to be evaluated. Taking the time to make certain the audits scope is clearly defined provides SAM leaders the opportunity to challenge or influence the manner in which discovery is executed and limit the requirement to use an auditor's scripts that likely produce far more detailed evidence than required to satisfy audit scope.

Define NDA Response

SAM leaders have shared with the SAM Optimization Council, now functioning as the ART, a summary of the Non-Disclosure Agreement language for each software publisher. An important agenda item for ART team members to consider is the appropriateness of the language for your enterprise and the manner in which the audit is to be carried out. The danger centers around the level of environment detail documented during the discovery process as many auditor scripts will generate far more discovery than required to identify non-compliance and potentially have the capability of sending information directly back to the auditor. If a third-party auditor is involved, traditional NDA's do not address the manner in which information will be shared between auditor and their client.

To address this three-way dynamic, *The SAM Leader Survival Guide* recommends the requirement for a trilateral NDA to ensure your information is used and managed for the specific audit scope.

Identify Entitlement Assembly Ownership

Reconciliation of discovery data against an accurate inventory of entitlements will be key to a successful audit outcome. SAM leaders have looked closely at the manner in which software is requested, approved and deployed in the organization and has defined the manner by which all entitlements are centralized in the SAM platform. Through this effort, entitlement management should be a straight forward activity. The ART should be assigned responsibility to go back to their respective areas and confirm new or in-process purchases.

Review Discovery Script Extract

A core ART activity will be to determine the exact output of the scripts and identify any potential environment impact, Information Security or privacy information concerns. This will be a joint effort of several ART team members to ensure if the auditors' scripts are utilized, the SAM leader fully understands the risk involved.

The SAM Leader Survival Guide will cover this again in the upcoming section on managing the audit. Forcing the auditor to accept liability for any issue the script can potentially cause is a tactic to slow the audit and provide the SAM leader and ART time to run an internal reconciliation in advance of data submission.

Review Deployment Profile

As part of ongoing education, SAM leaders have developed individual software publisher deployment profiles to help the IT organization better understand the dimensions necessary for an optimal environment. This information has been an ongoing part of reporting for the SAM Optimization Council. Now the ART team reviews this information for the specific publisher who has issued the audit to identify potential deployment breakdowns and remediation opportunities. The ART team member responsible for this area then checks and confirms with the team they have been maintaining appropriate diligence and to confirm compliance.

Identify Discovery POC

In addition to output from the SAM platform, it is advisable SAM leaders request the appropriate system generated reports for SAM analysts to triangulate data sources for enhanced accuracy prior to producing the data for an auditor's workbook. Once completed and any anomalies identified and remedied, it will be the SAM team's responsibility to pull the data and have the appropriate IT teams review and validate prior to submission.

Next, the assigned discovery POC compares data with the script output, if applicable, of the auditor to confirm gaps or unnecessary information to satisfy audit scope.

Review and Clarify Rules of Engagement

With receipt of an audit notification and assembly of the Audit Response Team, the level of interaction and communication with the software publisher must be modified to reflect the now formal relationship. The challenge will be that the software publisher account team will attempt to project no knowledge or involvement in the audit proceedings and want to proceed with a business as usual engagement. Internal teams, who are under pressure to deliver programs to support business transformation, will resist being told they are unable to interact with the publisher account and service teams.

SAM leaders need to jointly develop clear 'Rules of Engagement' for ART members to bring back to their organization. Failure to adhere to the agreed guidelines will only weaken an organization's ability to effectively manage and close the audit.

Review Communications Management

In addition to the external dynamics of an audit and proper engagement with representatives from the software publisher who has enacted their audit right, SAM leaders, via ART members, need to craft an internal communications strategy to help the organization remain focused and limit potential hysteria. SAM leaders need to help organizations craft a proper message regarding the audit and make certain the appropriate individuals are aware of the situation. Too many times SAM leaders attempt to sequester all information and keep those aware of the audit to a small handful of executives. This is a dangerous dynamic that ultimately places all liability for the audit on SAM operations and absolves all others from any involvement or accountability.

Formation and active utilization of the SAM Optimization Council, who is now functioning as the Audit Response Team due to the live audit, is a powerful means to ensure those who need to participate are aware of the audit with clear roles, responsibilities and accountabilities. Essentially 'calming the waters' and enabling a productive, coordinated audit response.

Review Publisher Susceptibility & Readiness

The SAM Leader Survival Guide will cover Publisher Susceptibility and Publisher Readiness shortly. These assets developed by the SAM leader are excellent documents that help reinforce ongoing audit readiness while identifying areas for potential improvement.

Reviewing this document with the ART helps bring focus to the areas where exposure may have continued to be identified by the software publisher as an audit target. Publisher Susceptibility and Publisher Readiness documents serve as a heat map for items the ART can potentially take emergency actions to remedy or reduce potential exposure before audit proceedings are formally underway.

Review Audit Workflow

Last, it is important SAM leaders provide ART members an overview of the probable phases of the audit. Individuals who are not close to or familiar with software audits may not fully understand the level of activity and length of time required to bring an audit to a successful conclusion. In addition, these same people need to understand the emotional rollercoaster a software audit triggers. It is important for SAM leaders to end or start each meeting with the exact point in the audit life cycle so ART team members have a full view of where in the audit life cycle they are and upcoming activities they will need to execute.

The SAM Leader Survival Guide has detailed these activities to help SAM leaders create internal confidence an organization is prepared for a software audit. Thinking like an auditor and anticipating the discovery areas focused on by professional auditors helps identify potential gaps and the steps necessary to remediate or optimize the environment. Utilizing the SAM Optimization Council as an ongoing advisory team enables SAM leaders to reinforce core SAM principles, creating a politically influential group fully prepared and rehearsed to support the requirements as the Audit Response Team. SAM leaders have carefully crafted the ART agenda to achieve alignment with the workings of the SAM Optimization Council to achieve effective, productive activity when an audit notification arrives.

SAM leaders now need to combine internal preparation with an insightful, ongoing analysis of external factors that can contribute to audit probability.

Audit Readiness – External Monitoring

Before we leave the subject of establishing and maintaining SAM audit- ready operations, it is important SAM leaders create the means to continually monitor potential audit exposure and specific characteristics that may contribute to making your organization an audit target. This is an area we continue to observe SAM leaders do not invest time and energy to develop, leading to unnecessary organizational paranoia pending audit exposure.

The SAM community views the primary item that draws a software publishers' attention to conduct an audit is merger and acquisition activity. We recognize this is a potential contributor for a software account team to target a firm, but it is not the only trigger that can shine a light on potential license non-compliance.

SAM leaders need to produce and maintain an assessment of their firm's potential audit exposure and audit readiness. Having a firm handle on each of the below identified areas enables SAM leaders to confidently address any internal questions that arise from executives as well as identify specific actions to reduce audit susceptibility and enhance readiness. This type of analysis is an excellent data point to review ongoing with the SAM Optimization Council and SAM Exec. SteerCo at each and every meeting.

Software Publisher Audit Susceptibility

When an organization receives an audit notification, the very first question from executives is 'why us'? The truth is there could be a number of reasons a firm is selected for audit and no matter how hard SAM leaders attempt to anticipate an audit, it is simply impossible to fully understand the motivation or specific factor that led to your organization being selected.

That said, SAM leaders must develop a method by which they can continually monitor and measure potential audit risk. It is the opinion of *The SAM Leader Survival Guide* there are multiple items that can heighten the potential for a firm being selected for audit. While many of the leading advisory firms point to mergers, acquisitions and divestitures as the primary trigger for audit, it is a mistake for SAM leaders to focus on this aspect alone and miss other factors which contribute to your organization being an audit candidate with software publishers account team and audit operation.

Before we take a look at the suggested items to assess your firms audit susceptibility, it is important to understand the role of the software publisher account team. Despite the typical response that they had no knowledge of a pending audit, account teams are highly influential in the selection of audit targets. As discussed previously in *The SAM Leader Survival Guide*, SAM leaders need to work diligently with sponsors, stakeholders, the Exec. SteerCo and the SAM Optimization Council to establish and maintain rules of engagement (RoE) for software publisher account teams. Account teams are measured on a number of criteria which drives their action to further penetrate and expand the business or miss their targets.

The following factors or dimensions are offered as a recommendation for SAM leaders when developing a simple calculator by which audit probability can be determined. Assigning a score of 1-10 with 1 being very low probability and 10 being high probability produces a quantifiable measure to determine which of the top software publishers in your environment pose the greatest threat. Each factor provides an opportunity to review current state and determine improvement tactics to lessen audit probability and improve SAM operations.

Factors to Assess Audit Susceptibility:

% of software spend

This metric is very important to account managers. Regardless of the raw spend a firm has with a specific publisher, every sales persons effectiveness is assessed based on percent of customer. As part of SAM operations reporting, SAM leaders are continually measuring top 10 publisher spend which percent of total software spend by publisher.

Annual Spend Trend

At a macro-level, SAM leaders can track year over year spend by publisher. Is it growing, flat or shrinking? Account managers will be measured by their leadership on these first two factors as the combination of the two are key indicators of a software publishers health and strategic relationship. If overall software spend is increasing and a publisher's revenue is flat to decreasing, sales team leadership will apply increasing pressure to the account team to remedy this challenge.

Publisher Account Team Stability

SAM leaders need to understand the full 'account management stack' of each strategic software partner. The goal is to have stability at mid to senior level account management for continuity with less focus of the 'on the ground' account manager. Is the team stable and do you have a relationship or is it a continuous revolving door? If there tends to be a significant level of change, these senior management roles may be more focused on quick wins to further their careers. Making an audit a possible tactic to stem perceived lost traction with your account is a possibility.

Publisher Ownership Stability

While we believe a firms merger and acquisition (M&A) activity is a lightning rod for an audit, the same can be true for recent change in the software publisher ownership structure. In particular when a publicly traded software firm is taken private with a significant investment from the Private Equity community, this signals a true bottom-line focus. As SAM leaders, we need to continually monitor the ownership structure of our strategic partners and perhaps even more importantly, the emerging software partners in our ecosystem.

IT Leadership Stability

Changes in IT leadership, at the CIO as well as VP and Director levels, can be a contributor to software publishers targeting a firm for an audit. In particular if they fear roadmap and transformation alignment or if there is a past history between the publisher and executive that was less than positive. SAM leaders have the opportunity to develop forums in which publisher account teams have strategic briefings that will help those account teams feel connected and see potential for emerging opportunities. This will cause account teams to take a pause if the discussion of audit is raised within their organization.

Merger, Acquisition & Divestiture Activity

Yes M&A activity appears to be a trigger for audits. At the core, some account team is being impacted, leading to the recommendation that a client is audited. In addition, most organizations struggle with the concept of assignments making the probability very high that non-compliance exists during the transitionary period. The means to minimize the impact of an audit is diligence of entitlement management and clarity regarding assignment rights and conditions associated with the event.

Roadmap Alignment

This is closely aligned with 'share of customer'. Account managers sense emerging opportunities and if they see their position is weakening and not aligned with the direction of a customer, they may invoke an audit in an attempt to leverage findings into a purchase.

Renewal History

Have recent renewals been a challenge? What were the dynamics? When considering this dimension SAM leaders need to understand that even a software spend that is increasing may not be sufficient to make the renewal an easy, straight forward engagement. If the account team is disappointed and these discussions have been a bit contentious, the probability of audit increases.

Periodic Reporting Requirement Status

IBM set the stage in this area with the requirement for use of the IBM License Management Tool (ILMT) sub-capacity PVU-based metric quarterly reporting requirement. Oracle, SAP and others are attempting to introduce similar requirements. SAM leaders need to track adherence and accuracy of these items or they can have a damaging impact if audited. This factor needs to be considered in both 'audit susceptibility' as well as 'audit readiness' as maintenance of these tools are challenging.

Deployment Discipline

As a focus of the SAM Optimization Council, it is important to include a measure of deployment effectiveness in assessing audit susceptibility. Account Managers, using insight potentially gained by the implementation support teams based on any change in volume, will have a sense as to an organizations discipline. If an IT operations team and SAM team appear to have detailed knowledge of use rights, license requirements with continual reporting, account team members will pick-up on this and communicate internally that a client's environment appears well managed.

Contract Changes

There are multiple dynamics in an enterprise agreement that can be revised and change over time. If there has been significant contractual change this can also be an item to draw the attention of the account team leading to a potential audit.

Account Team Onsite Presence

Previously, we outlined the concept of rules of engagement (RoE) as an important element to effectively manage a software publishers or resellers account teams. This specific item for susceptibility regards the level and type of access these individuals have to your facility. Freedom to move enables account teams to pick up not only on many of the items covered in this susceptibility list, but also gain insight to potential upcoming projects or deployment gaps. Access needs to be controlled and orchestrated with IT teams.

IT Executive Access

Account teams are pressured to demonstrate to their leadership that they have close, effective influence with senior IT leaders.

They will press to gain access and learn future plans. If they do not have access or are being shut out, concern grows. Again, as part of the SAM leaders' overall rules of engagement, account teams with strategic partners need to have coordinated access to IT leaders.

Audit History

Considering the past audit history is helpful especially if the outcome was incorporated into a lesson learned approach and audit findings were helpful in driving internal improvement. *The SAM Leader Survival Guide* finds organizations that were audited and there were substantial findings. If little has changed outwardly in terms of SAM execution, the potential for audit is high.

Creating and maintaining an audit susceptibility calculator or tracker is intended to be an item owned by SAM leaders. Use the SAM Optimization Council as a sounding board, but this is a self-evaluation that SAM leaders should have at the ready. Of the list provided, select those items that best align to your organization and assemble the initial calculation. This simple exercise and subsequent scoring are a strong contributor to help calm an organization's audit concerns and bring laser focus to items that can be controlled.

Software Publisher Audit Readiness

SAM leaders need to be very careful and not simply speak of audit exposure or susceptibility. It is very important to provide an equally important counterbalance that reinforces SAM operational audit readiness. Developing this tool enables SAM leaders to focus the SAM Optimization Council and Exec. SteerCo members on specific actions to improve readiness, enhancing the perception that SAM operations are effectively identifying and mitigating risk.

Like an audit susceptibility calculator, SAM leaders should create an excel spreadsheet that outlines the below factors assigning an individual score per item. Again, the approach is to score each factor on a scale of 1 to 10 with 1 being low readiness and 10 being exceptional or high readiness. In this manner, the factors with low scores present an opportunity to explore improvement tactics and recommendation with the SAM Optimization Council. When combined with the audit susceptibility scoring, SAM leaders are able to identify those publishers who present the greatest risk and the steps necessary to improve audit readiness.

Factors to Assess Audit Readiness:

Audit Language

The items identified for determining audit readiness by software publisher align with many of the recommended agenda items SAM leaders will utilize for the SAM Optimization Council. The difference here is that developing a single summary and assigning an individual score per item enables SAM leaders to quickly identify areas of opportunity for reinforcement and those that are seen to be strong.

Assessing the audit language of each major software publisher enables SAM leaders to determine the level of effort or challenge if an audit is enacted and quickly do a side by side comparison. Make certain audit time requirements are clear, documented and understood.

A common recommendation from advisory firms in this area is for organizations to negotiate away the ability of the software publisher to invoke an audit. While this can prove to be a positive outcome, *The SAM Leader Survival Guide* believes a focus on removing audit rights can create the impression an organization is non-compliant. When the negotiated grace period comes to an end, it is a near certainty the audit notification will arrive. An alternative is to focus on discovery data source and securing the right for submission of the SAM operations preferred reporting. This type of negotiation subtly informs the software publisher that a SAM operation exists and is ready for an audit when required. The likely outcome will be that your organization falls to the bottom of the list when audit targets are being identified.

NDA

The element to consider with the Non-disclosure agreement is readiness. An understanding of the NDA language in the enterprise agreement and how the team will respond with a 3-way NDA or another agreed approach is based on SAM Optimization Council input.

Deployment Capability

SAM leaders need to utilize their insight to subjectively score the level of deployment discipline or effectiveness for each strategic publisher. The data points to utilize will be a combination of the discussions held with the SAM Optimization Council as well as data from the SAM platform tracking deployment effectiveness. In addition, SAM leaders need to continually monitor the level of support calls, as an increase in this area can tip-off an account team that a client is having trouble or there has been an increase in deployment. If the account team does not see a corresponding increase in orders, they will increase their efforts to gain insight to the environment.

License Knowledge

SAM operations need to take proactive measures to educate the teams on the various license implications by publisher, by product, by environment (physical, virtual, cloud etc.). Through this effort, combined with the information shared with the SAM Optimization Council, SAM leaders will have a good understanding of the complexity by publisher and the ability of the team to not only understand, but using SAM platform analysis, their ability to execute.

Entitlement Management

It is surprising how many times we have observed SAM operations and Sourcing struggle to maintain accurate, complete and up to date records of license ownership. Upgrade and downgrade rights and other dynamics unique to software agreements challenge teams to have the necessary confidence to effectively reconcile against deployment. Each publisher presents different nuances based upon their specific use rights, license requirements, enterprise agreements terms and conditions. To assess audit readiness, SAM leaders need to consider these dynamics and determine how effective current processes are combined with an assessment of how quickly entitlements can be confirmed if an audit was enacted.

Rules of Engagement Effectiveness

We have mentioned in several different areas the importance of defining and adhering to a predefined, structured methodology by which internal teams interact with software publishers. If teams adhere to these standards, not only does it reduce the potential for account teams to request and implement friendly optimization assessments (soft audit), it supports audit readiness as the likelihood the account teams have learned information that could compromise an audit response is reduced.

Utilizing Audit Susceptibility & Readiness Calculators

SAM leaders are urged to maintain audit susceptibility and readiness measures in a format that enables quick and easy consumption across SAM's sponsors, stakeholders and the teams developed to support SAM operations. While each item to measure susceptibility and readiness outlined in the preceding sections are subjective, assigning a score and totaling the results enables SAM leaders to show quantitative measurement in a clean, easy to consume format. Used in conjunction, the two calculators enable SAM leaders to speak to those software publishers who present the most likely probability of audit and the measures or steps necessary to improve readiness in the event an audit is enacted. This is a powerful combination by which SAM leaders can build confidence and calm internal audit anxiety.

Part 4 – Audit Ready SAM Operations – Summary

Part 4 has provided SAM leaders a detailed game plan by which to establish and maintain audit readiness. It is not required to implement each and every recommendation, however *The SAM Leader Survival Guide* strongly suggests that knowledge of each element with an understanding of how to apply the tactics enables SAM leaders to align with their organization's unique requirements.

We are now ready to respond effectively to receipt of an audit notification as the team is prepared. Now SAM leaders need to carefully consider how to best manage internal dynamics while the audit is in process. Failure to do so, despite establishing string audit ready capabilities, can leave SAM leaders isolated and vulnerable.

Part 5 – Internal Audit Dynamics: 'The Game Within the Game!'

Now that we have established audit ready SAM operations and built the required relationships with an empowered cross-functional SAM Optimization Council, SAM leaders need to deliver a well-defined, pre-determined game plan when notified of an audit notification. There are dozens of resources SAM leaders can turn to that provide step by step breakdown of the activities or workflow of a software audit. *The SAM Leader Survival Guide* will not attempt to duplicate or repeat this readily available information covering the interaction between auditor and auditee. The goal of this section is to identify the internal undercurrent and dynamics SAM leaders must effectively manage, or suffer severe reputational impact. Our goal is to analyze 'the game within the game' so SAM leaders can anticipate events and take preemptive measures for internal challenges.

Executive Audit Anxiety

It is a natural reaction for SAM leaders to focus on the issue at hand: proper audit management and response execution. However, we have found SAM leaders need to apply equal focus to internal issues to manage expectations and quickly resolve issues. It is at this point that SAM leaders need to anticipate what executives are asking one another and stating in private. While there is a logical, step by step audit process SAM leaders can employ, there is also a predictable progression of questions executives will want SAM leaders to address in order to assess exposure. SAM leaders who can anticipate and take pre-emptive steps will help reduce anxiety across executives. We have captured the flow of the typical questions below to serve as a guide for SAM leaders to prepare specific measures designed to manage internal stress while maintaining the needed focus on a successful audit outcome.

"Why Us?"

This is a common immediate response across executives when an audit notification is delivered. Remember, under the surface, executives believe the investment in SAM operations is an insurance policy to prevent audits. It is this foundational perspective that SAM leaders must address and continuously emphasize the need for audit ready operations. Creation of the SAM Mission and Value statement, close interaction and management of sponsors and stakeholders, along with formation of the SAM Exec SteerCo and SAM Optimization Council, are all engineering to help SAM leaders establish the focus on audit readiness and not audit prevention.

With receipt of the audit notification, the SAM Optimization Council transforms to the Audit Response Team. SAM leaders immediately package all of the analysis for the specific software publisher to produce the 'Audit Playbook' covering audit language, audit scope, NDA response plan, discovery assignments, potential remediation or clean-up activities along with audit communications and roadmap of anticipated activities. SAM Susceptibility and SAM Readiness calculators quickly enable SAM leaders to turn the discussion to specifics, producing focus and targeted actions to remedy the hysteria.

Do not underestimate the impact of this question becoming a point of discussion in senior executive meetings. The better prepared SAM's executive and peripheral sponsors, the more quickly this lingering question will be addressed. Make certain your sponsors are well prepared.

"What's Our Exposure?"

The next immediate question from executives will be a demand to quantify the audits potential exposure in terms of financial impact. SAM leaders need to be very, very careful as whatever the quoted number is, it will boomerang back and impact credibility. *The SAM Leader Survival Guide* urges SAM leaders to avoid the desire to state potential exposure in terms of dollars and instead, point to what is known. Use the readiness calculator and susceptibility calculator to identify strengths, weaknesses and outline the high-level audit game plan.

If you are not successful and are cornered into stating a potential exposure, attempt to state a range versus a hard figure. The following typical scenarios tend to unfold requiring careful consideration as none are good for SAM leaders.

SAM leader states high financial impact – Many times a SAM leader will provide leadership a high estimated audit judgement with the goal of being conservative. As an example, the SAM leader states that potential audit findings can be in the $1 to $1.5 million range. When the draft preliminary finding is delivered by the auditor identifying the initial amount of $500,000.00, instead of executives being relieved, they question the SAM leader's capability.

SAM leader estimates a low impact – At other times, the SAM leader does not want to cause unnecessary internal stress and will quote a modest anticipated judgement amount. As an example, the SAM leader states that potential audit findings can be in the $500,000 to $750,000 range. When the draft preliminary findings are delivered by the auditor identifying a non-compliance amount of $1.5 million, once again, executives will question the SAM leader's capability.

Be careful! In many ways this is a no-win situation for SAM leaders. Executives will lock onto the initial number quoted by SAM leaders and use it as the baseline for all future discussions. SAM leaders need to understand this fact and continually provide a detailed breakdown that always starts with the original quoted amount and then a step by step 'walk' back with the specific items that have reduced or increased the exposure. In this manner, SAM leaders always start with the original number and show expertise in how we have arrived at current estimates with identification of those actions and tactics that have reduced potential exposure

For example, you as the SAM leader, may be pressed by your CIO and CFO to give an initial estimate of potential exposure, with the assurance that it is understood you won't be held accountable until more is known (which never happens). With this agreed condition in place, you state initial estimated exposure could be in the $3million range. From this point forward, all reporting on estimated exposure must start with the initial estimate of $3 million and detail the exact items that produced the reduction. Picture a waterfall-style chart that shows the initial $3 million and then the specific reduction amount per item leading to the final, new estimated exposure.

Surprisingly, many SAM leaders are forced into a position of guessing when they should be developing the detailed financial impact of the auditor's draft ELP. While the ELP will not have prices, it will identify licenses consumed by product. Perhaps the draft ELP will include entitlement level by product, but if not, SAM leaders and their teams should be able to take the draft ELP and add a column indicating number of licenses owned. By doing so, SAM leaders can identify license delta by product. With this documented, multiply the delta by the current price for that product minus the current EA discount. This will provide SAM leaders a solid basis on which to define potential exposure as well as prioritize the negotiation and auditor challenge tactics.

The subject of audit exposure will now be part of every interaction between the CIO, IT finance and the CFO. Be prepared! The CFO will likely be demanding the CIO quantify exposure and report updates on an ongoing basis. The CIO, anticipating the CFO's request, will be demanding continuous updates of remediation and exposure estimates. Due to this pressure, your CIO may be pushing to get involved directly with the software publisher with the belief they can negotiate away the audit. SAM leaders need to be sensitive to these internal dynamics and be prepared to help calm leaders while the Audit Response Team swings into action in a calm, coordinated manner.

"Who else do we need to worry about?"

While SAM leaders are attempting to keep the ART team and executives focused to execute the required comprehensive audit response, the very natural next question executives will be asking behind closed doors is 'who else do we need to be concerned about?'. SAM leaders who have taken the time to develop and maintain the audit susceptibility and readiness calculators will have the analysis necessary to quickly respond to these comments, build executive confidence and maintain focus on the audit at hand. If not, SAM operations will be distracted as they need to field a series of fragmented questions and be required to respond in some manner in an attempt to calm executive concern. Clearly this distracts from the core mission of achieving an effective audit response.

SAM leaders, knowing this dynamic will occur, despite every effort to address this through the SAM Exec. SteerCo and SAM Optimization Council, need to be at the ready. This is a critical period of time for SAM leaders, requiring the ability to effectively manage the audit and effectively influence internal dynamics that can either bring positive focus to SAM operations or adversely impact credibility.

"How much should we accrue?"

Closely aligned with executive demands for knowing what the potential exposure may be, IT finance will begin to question the SAM leader on how much to accrue in order to mitigate financial impact. Again, this is very challenging for SAM leaders as the amount quoted will be documented with any variance, positive or negative, projecting a poor impression on SAM operations. As part of the SAM Optimization Council now functioning as the ART, IT finance should understand the audit workflow and pending draft ELP. However, SAM leaders need to be very proactive to reinforce with IT finance the dramatic variances that likely will be experienced, and the number will be somewhat fluid.

"We're out of compliance by how much????"

Despite the SAM leaders' best efforts to educate the SAM Exec. SteerCo and the SAM Optimization Council inclusive of IT finance, an auditors preliminary or draft effective license position (ELP) will be grossly inflated. This again presents significant challenges for SAM leaders and can have serious impact to their credibility.

Prior to discovery data submission, SAM operations in collaboration with the ART, have validated the accuracy of the data with reconciliation against current license entitlements to develop an assessment of any potential non-compliance. During the window of time between submission to the auditor and receipt of the draft ELP, tension begins to build. This is a time the SAM leader needs to calmly communicate auditor draft preliminary findings are notoriously inflated, based on assumptions, interpretations that favor the software publisher. Preparing the team in advance will help reduce the emotional rollercoaster that's about to occur.

Preliminary ELP results typically show the number of licenses being utilized by product, or perhaps the delta license count between owned and deployed licenses. Rarely will the auditor put pricing or exposure until the final ELP is produced. While this is a negotiation tactic for the auditor, SAM leaders need to carefully add to the draft ELP a column indicating the current price per license for each product identified in the ELP and multiply by the delta. This should be done for both over and under deployed products for a complete view of potential puts and takes. By taking this action, SAM leaders quantify total exposure and ensure prioritization of those areas producing the greatest impact. Now the ART can work in a focused manner to address findings, producing the needed evidence to satisfy or challenge the auditor's determination.

Reporting to the CIO and CFO at this time needs to be aligned with the SAM leaders initial quoted potential exposure and again utilize a waterfall style approach to show the challenge strategy for each major finding. Findings will reduce over the span of several rounds with back and forth auditor interactions. SAM leaders need to make certain the team understands that working each issue with the required level of detail and focus will ultimately produce favorable results, but it will take time.

"We will settle this with the Software Vendor!"

Over the period of time in which the ART and SAM leader is working with the auditor, there are no negotiations. This is the process by which the auditor will determine if the evidence provided satisfies their request and eliminates or reduces the specific finding. Through this process, SAM leaders have focused on addressing the interpretations and assumptions applied by the auditors along with identification of opportunities for optimization of the environment to reduce the identified exposure.

Back and forth discussions occur over an extended period in which the audit has moved from preliminary findings to the final audit findings report which will be provided to the software publisher. It is at this time negotiations kick into focus, not before.

This is a very important point for SAM leaders to understand and take proactive measures to ensure senior executives know when they will be called upon to secure a successful, final settlement. Due to the visibility of the audit and high-stakes involved, executives naturally want to be engaged and leverage the 'relationship' card to achieve a quick outcome. SAM leaders need to continually outline the strategy for ongoing communications with executives, identifying when the executive will be engaged and what their expected role will be. By maintaining control, SAM leaders are able to utilize executive support at the best possible time to secure the desired outcome. It also helps reinforce for the executives that SAM operations are effective at leading and managing an audit from initiation to closure.

"Aren't we done?"

The importance of properly closing out an audit proceeding is never evident until the next audit. By the time an audit reaches the final stages and a settlement is in final negotiations, the ART and SAM Exec. SteerCo are exhausted and simply want to bring the proceedings to an end. It is at this point SAM leaders need to remain diligent and keep the team focused as 3rd party auditor and software publishers may not properly document concessions and agreed remedies. Many times, these items are only documented in an email from the account manager versus ensuring proper documentation and revisions to the enterprise agreement. This unfortunate approach leads to challenges if and when a follow-up audit is executed or a contentious renewal occurs.

SAM leaders need to make certain to rally the team and ensure appropriate documentation, including audit closure, any remedies that satisfy identified findings, along with any agreed, negotiated positions reflected as net new language in the EA or as a formal addendum. Software publisher account teams change over frequently. It is important SAM teams do not rely on e-mails or a handshake to close an audit. Not following thru only exposes a client to future audit and potential claims that the previously agreed negotiated settlement was not successfully implemented, reopening what was thought to be closed.

"How do we prevent this in the future?"

Everyone knows the value of conducting post-mortem review sessions and incorporating lessons learned for future benefit. As the audit is officially closed and final reports are produced, ART members are tired and want to move on. Members of the Exec. SteerCo are also worn out by the length of time to close the audit and the emotional rollercoaster they have experienced, yet it is at this exact time that SAM leaders need to hold a detailed lessons learned session and identify any improvements to be incorporated into SAM operations as well as other areas where process breakdowns contributed to audit findings.

The internal team who has dealt with the most significant challenges has been IT finance and the CFO, due to the potential impact to financial reporting requirements. This team will want to know what IT and SAM are going to do to prevent the level of internal disturbance in the future. "How can we better determine the exposure?" "How can we better determine accrual levels?" "What can we do to eliminate audits?"

As SAM leaders, we know the importance of supporting these questions but need to continually speak in terms of ranges and where in the audit process we are. We need to revise the confidence factor from +/- 50% to +/- 25% when we have studied the auditors draft ELP and can better assess a potential range of exposure. Subsequently we should move to a confidence factor of 80% when SAM has eliminated portions of the targeted findings based on evidence submitted and correction of incorrect interpretations or auditor assumptions.

SAM leaders have the opportunity at this point to produce an 'Audit Response Assessment' style document, reinforce lessons learned, and recommend tactics to reduce internal disruption when the next audit arrives.

Executive Stress Reduction

Now that we can anticipate the natural drama that unfolds for executives when a software audit is underway, SAM leaders can develop the appropriate game plan sensitive to the tendencies of the internal 'game within the game'. Building upon the relationship with the SAM Exec. SteerCo and SAM Optimization Council, SAM leaders need to recognize the heightened need for proactive communications to ensure all involved fully understand the exact audit status, upcoming milestones, and areas of identified exposure with targeted remediation or challenge strategies.

At this time, the SAM Optimization Council is functioning as the Audit Response Team so SAM leaders need to concentrate the following guidance on the Exec. SteerCo and other critical executives such as the CFO or CPO who may not be part of the ongoing team.

Audit Awareness Plan

SAM leaders, recognizing the need for effective and frequent audit status communications should leverage multiple techniques and forums to ensure the information is getting through the executive noise-level. While simple, *The SAM Leader Survival Guide* continues to observe SAM leaders' reaction to an audit notification is to keep those aware of the audit to a select few individuals. It is our opinion this tendency causes SAM leaders unnecessary complications as anxiety builds and rumors begin to spread. SAM leaders must be highly aware and sensitive to the internal stress and anxiety that builds and use the following tactics to keep a pulse on executive dynamics.

Audit Executive Committee

Slightly different than the standing SAM Exec. SteerCo, the Audit Executive Committee should be expanded to include the software publishers executive sponsor and greater participation from IT finance. This team will be critical as SAM leaders work though the ebb and flow of audit phases.

Meetings

SAM leaders need to educate the Audit Executive Committee on scheduled meeting times aligned to the level of activity for the specific audit phase. Typically, every-other week or monthly quick targeted sessions will help ensure these individuals are fully aware of the exact status and upcoming milestones. Normally the meetings are more frequent at the outset, slow as the auditor is developing the draft effective license position (ELP) and then become more frequent once again upon receipt of the draft ELP for review and validation of audit defense strategies.

Written Updates

With an e-mail or a quick PowerPoint summary attached to a mail (as required), SAM leaders maintain an open and ongoing scheduled dialogue with the team. This will help reduce the need for more face to face meetings and provide the recipient an opportunity to forward as they see appropriate.

One-on-One Meetings

SAM leaders need to maintain a schedule of one on one meetings with key members and influencers of the Audit Executive Committee. These are the individuals a SAM leader wants to ensure have a firm handle on all the information and who understands the required actions and those who need to act in order to minimize audit impact.

Part 5 – Internal Audit Dynamics – Summary

The focus of *The SAM Leader Survival Guide* section on audit management tendencies has been understanding internal dynamics of executives when an audit is underway to help SAM leaders anticipate levels of anxiety and stress building below the surface. By doing so, SAM leaders are in an excellent position to maintain the focus of the ART while managing executive concerns. Failure to do so can have a profound impact on SAM operational confidence by the executives who made the investment decision. Conversely, proactive measures in this area will cement the SAM leader's capability with key executives.

Part 6 – Cloud: The Future is Here

Cloud computing has been a topic of conversation for the past 10 years or more. It appears its time has finally arrived, and cloud computing has become the leading means by which organizations are transforming operations to provide digital capabilities. The initial perception was that movement to the cloud will simplify software asset management and in fact could eliminate the need for such a function. While this impression may persist in certain circles, as cloud offerings have diversified to include software as a service (SaaS), infrastructure as a service (IaaS) and platform as a service (PaaS) capabilities, governance and overall management of cloud is proving a challenge for most firms. In addition to exposure to license compliance issues, IT executives are increasingly looking to SAM leaders to help fill several critical functions to improve cloud governance and efficiency.

Cloud Center of Excellence

As usual, Gartner has been a leader in digging into the emerging challenges of governing hybrid cloud environments. While a good deal of focus can be spent on the need to manage shadow IT activities, the shortfall in governance of cloud assets is becoming a CIO pain point as ineffective cloud management produces significant unbudgeted impact. In response to this dynamic, many organizations are establishing a Cloud Center of Excellence (CCOE). However, SAM leaders need to avoid the mistake of assuming the CCOE will own all aspects of cloud management across a complete life cycle. Gartner projects that organizations typically have 30% of cloud assets that are toxic consumption. Toxic consumption means that cloud capacity or subscription not in use yet are invoiced each and every month. Is this the role of the CCOE to manage? Vendor Management? Software Asset Management? Telecom Expense Management (TEM) or other?

We have observed CCOE's tend to focus on what can be called the 'front-end' of cloud activities and quickly distance themselves from 'back-end' activities. SAM leaders need to fully understand the role and responsibility of an organizations CCOE to clarify accountability and authority. Forcing this level of discussion across IT leaders will reduce misunderstandings and unmet expectations when issues around governance, utilization levels and efficiency arise, which they will.

While the scope and focus of a CCOE will shift from organization to organization, *The SAM Leader Survival Guide* has observed several items that appear consistently across the cloud community. Even if there is no formal CCOE at your organization as yet, the below functions are likely being performed within IT infrastructure operations. SAM leaders need to be proactive in understanding the what, when, and who elements to fully appreciate the internal cloud landscape.

Cloud Center of Excellence – Typical Areas of Focus
Cloud Service Provider (CSP) Negotiation

From the start, sourcing and procurement teams have been challenged to keep up with IT organizations and functional business units as they engage Cloud Service Providers (CSP). Initial agreements may have been concluded with little focus on software implications, service level agreements, or access to the information necessary to monitor usage.

Cloud Architecture Definition

In many respects, the central role of a CCOE is to determine the appropriate cloud architecture versions for their organizations to ensure optimal performance and appropriate information security. Working closely with the CSP's, the CCOE ensures the technical offerings are defined and documented.

Cloud Workload Design & Support

With the definition of approved architecture, the CCOE turns to educating internal teams and helping various business units identify areas of their environment that are cloud-ready or those that, with moderate modification, can be moved. In many respects, this is a marketing activity as the CCOE is incentivized to maximize use of the cloud.

CSP Comparison/Selection

With identification of workload ready to move to the cloud, the CCOE may help the team determine which CSP provides the best technical offering and efficiency. Today, most organizations have a hybrid cloud environment preferring to utilize a portfolio of CSPs with the goal of having flexibility and retaining a perceived level of leverage.

CSP Relationship Management

Leadership of the CCOE will play a central role in CSP relationship management. CCOE acts as the primary interface and seeks support from the CSP to help transition a growing cloud footprint across the organization.

It is *The SAM Leader Survival Guide's* opinion that many organizations have potential exposure when it comes to comprehensive, integrated governance of cloud environments. While IT leaders will inform all they have established a Cloud Center of Excellence, governance, management of subscription levels and usage remain a lesser priority. Many times, the metrics by which the CCOE is being measured is a disincentive for them to track utilization as their focus is on growing cloud footprint.

This presents an opportunity for SAM leaders to become a part of the CCOE as a significant contributor or take control of a Cloud Asset Manager (CAM) function. Currently, the concept of a Cloud Asset Manager function is being promoted by several leading analyst firms. What is not clear is where this function best resides within the organization. Some believe it to be a CCOE responsibility while others promote leveraging the capabilities of organizations expert in areas such as contract management, invoice verification and relationship management.

The below areas are potential opportunities for SAM leaders to support a CCOE or IT infrastructure teams by stepping in and performing the following critical cloud governance activities.

Cloud Center of Excellence - Typical Delegated Task
Utilization Verification

Utilization can be measured in a number of ways. Gartner estimates that 30% of all cloud consumption is unused or nonproductive. The term they use for this is 'toxic' consumption for Infrastructure as a Service (IaaS) and Platform as a Service (PaaS) where the resources are provisioned, yet inactive. Unused SaaS licenses also are placed into this category.

In this period of cloud hypergrowth, some CCO's do not view utilization as a core focus. The CCOE is focused on supporting teams by identifying the workloads, process by which they move to the cloud, and ensuring initial implementations align with cloud and information security standards.

SAM leaders have the opportunity to support their organization by taking on the accountability to track, analyze and report utilization across a number of dimensions. This insight will prove invaluable in helping avoid compliance issues for IaaS and PaaS and provide SAM leaders the opportunity to develop deep expertise on spend and utilization dynamics across all flavors of cloud.

It is impossible to leave this subject without discussing challenges related to SaaS subscription measurement and optimization. This is a discipline that has grown significantly more complex since the initial user-based metric. No organization depicts this evolution better than Salesforce.com.

SAM leaders need to ensure they are engaged in negotiations and governance of this rapidly growing provider of SaaS-based cloud services. We have observed Salesforce.com is consistently becoming a Top 10 spend for most organizations and cracking the Top 5 for annual spend in many. Salesforce.com provides a myriad of licensing models and use-metrics that present a challenge for most organizations to effectively manage and optimize. While audits are not typical with SaaS providers as they maintain complete records of your organization's consumption, SAM leaders need to step in and support negotiations with optimized metrics, or organizations will continue to pay a premium for Salesforce. com services. Based on size of spend and breadth of Salesforce. com services and platforms, a fulltime associate dedicated to measurement and internal reporting may be required.

Invoice Verification

The SAM Leader Survival Guide has yet to find a CCOE that diligently reviews monthly invoices for accuracy via the CSP provided portals. This is a complex, time consuming, and thankless task that has existed for years in the world of Telecom Expense Management (TEM) as these teams have had to continually verify invoices across multiple carriers.

In a cloud setting, much of this information is readily available through portals, but confirming dates implemented, dates removed and to ensure the automated calculations are accurate is challenging. With SaaS, IaaS and PaaS cloud components, there is also some level of knowledge required to ensure the specific cloud category invoices are accurate.

While not a natural extension for SAM leaders, when aligned with utilization verification, a more complete picture of spend and underlying trends emerge. This is excellent information for SAM leaders to leverage and drive internal awareness with proactive forecasting and targeted recommendations.

SLA Management

Typically managed by a Vendor Management organization (VMO), service level agreements (SLAs) are designed to monitor the level of service provided by each CSP. While the CCOE will likely claim accountability for this task, true diligence on measuring and reporting SLAs in advance of service impact is lacking. First generation Cloud Agreements, specifically SaaS services, typically have limited to no real consequence for CSP's in the event of service degradation or complete downtime. Where IT datacenter environments have expected uptime in the 99.999% uptime range, many cloud service levels may be 95% or best efforts.

This is an area SAM leader should be aware of and remain informed about, but allow others more expert in this discipline to chime in. As Gartner has stated very effectively, SAM leaders should be focused on toxic consumption and potential license non-compliance due to the complexities associated with Bring Your Own License (BYOL) and the various CSP schemes.

Software License Management

The SAM Leader Survival Guide will cover this in a bit more detail shortly. However, as it relates to the accountability of the CCOE, SAM leaders need to be aware that this is not an area of great focus or expertise due to the various conversion schemes and metrics associated with porting licenses to the cloud as well as the surrounding use rights. SAM operations need to step in and support this need.

Cloud Transformation

Closely aligned with license use rights and the complex maze of requirements, SAM leaders and their teams need to carefully monitor the concept of 'dual-use'. This is when an 'on-premise' environment remains in production while the cloud-equivalent is being established. Each software publisher has rules for BYOL for IaaS and PaaS in terms of the length of time acceptable for these to run in parallel. Exceeding these time limits can have a dramatic impact on a firm's compliance posture if audited by the software publisher. This is an area SAM leaders need to push aggressively to own as part of contributing to the CCOE's metrics.

Physical Environment Closure

Measurement of 'dual-use' timeframe is necessary not only for license exposure but to track the decommissioning and removal of the on-premise environment. In addition to potential audit findings, delayed removal of the legacy environments has a compounding impact to the IT budget.

SAM leaders, working in collaboration with Hardware Asset Management (HAM) and the IT Asset Management team can ensure efficiency is achieved, or shine the spotlight on unnecessary cost.

Cloud Implications For SAM

It is important for SAM leaders to take time and assess their organizations approach to cloud management. While we have focused the above comments on an internal cloud center of excellence, if a CCOE does not exist in name, there are individuals in IT or individual business units who are on point for the functions described above. It is recommended SAM leaders hold a series of interviews and participate in sessions focused on cloud strategy and operational execution to identify areas where SAM can add value while mitigating risk and reducing toxic consumption.

Just like many executives view their investment in Software Asset Management as audit insurance, many of these same individuals assume the movement to cloud capabilities will reduce or eliminate the threat of software audits. Clearly this raises a vulnerability to a SAM operation. SAM leaders who take the time to study CCOE typical functions, their current focus and level of performance, will be able to identify areas where SAM operations, leveraging SAM core knowledge, can expand the SAM mission and become a valued contributor to cloud governance.

When we take the time to separate cloud activities into two, broad buckets with one focused on technical implications and the other focused on governance and optimization, it typically becomes clear that organizations benefit from a broader, cross-functional, multi-skilled team involved with cloud life cycle management. During the initial stages when cloud was being piloted and initial strategies developed, it was appropriate to have an isolated team of technology experts fully dedicated to developing the organizational cloud strategy. With cloud now becoming mainstream with an increasing percent of corporate computing on the platform, SAM leaders can bring value while identifying and reducing risk in the form of greater governance diligence.

SAM Sponsor & Stakeholder Alignment

With completion of internal study on the various cloud elements being performed within your organization, SAM leaders document the specific value SAM operations can bring to effective governance of cloud. Not only to preserve software license exposure, but to bring the analyst skills to support utilization and consumption management.

With the basic position defined, SAM leaders need to subtly work across SAM's sponsors and stakeholders to explain the identified cloud governance gaps, the manner in which SAM operations can address these gaps and the value produced though effective monitoring and proactive management of these gaps.

Mission Statement - Cloud

With successful engagement of SAM's sponsors and stakeholders, revise the SAM Mission Statement and execute the recommended communications tactics previously described in the 'Building a Sustainable SAM Operation' section.

Value Statement - Cloud

Quantify the value SAM operations will bring to effective cloud governance beyond the management of porting BYOL to IaaS and PaaS applications and SaaS subscription maintenance. Combined with effective reporting to sponsors and stakeholders providing insight to cloud spend trends and emerging observations, SAM operations now have the opportunity to be part of the digital future.

Cloud Center of Excellence Member

Successful discussions with sponsors and stakeholders will enable SAM to become a formal part of the established CCOE or participate in meetings with those who are providing the function. In fact, if your organization does not as yet have a dedicated CCOE, SAM leaders can help executives see the value of creating one. In essence, SAM leaders can drive the need to better govern the downstream of backend implications of cloud adoption.

The SAM Cloud Game Plan

SAM leaders have several natural targets in which their SAM operations can bring value to their organization's governance of cloud. Some items are a direct area of responsibility such as BYOL, but many are peripheral or related areas where SAM can bring insight and expertise. *The SAM Leader Survival Guide* has identified a few such areas below, however this is not intended to be an exhaustive list. Each organization is different and at a specific point of cloud maturity, these suggestions need to be adjusted to align with your environment. These items are intended to form the basis or foundation for SAM operations contribution to cloud governance.

Cloud Policy & Control Definition

SAM leaders have great expertise in the development of formal 'policy' and supporting 'controls' to reduce the purchase of non-conforming items. Leveraging what has been previously described in the section 'Building A Sustainable SAM Operation', SAM leaders can work with legal, sourcing, ITSM, executives and members of the CCOE to develop policy by which the organization can engage Cloud Service Providers, validating that the CSP service meets predefined guidelines and process by which contracting and procurement are executed. In essence, the upfront, onboarding is defined and managed, thereby reducing organization and operational risk. This will yield a series of outputs in the form of documents and workflows for the required approvals while at the same time providing SAM operations excellent visibility.

Cloud Transformation Intelligence

IT organizations are under pressure to adopt 'cloud first' mentality. This pressure forces teams to move workload to the cloud and they may not have full knowledge of the elements that can determine efficiency. We do not believe SAM operations should be involved with assessing compliance of CCOE predefined architecture.

Instead SAM should focus on providing teams effective summaries of requirements associated with transitioning environments to a cloud platform. Development of these easy to consume assets, combined with some coaching, will establish SAM as a valued partner on cloud issues.

CSP Terms & Conditions Summary

Each cloud service provider and software publisher have specific terms and conditions associated with 'transition-in' of a workload as well as 'transition out' of the cloud platform, whether it be IaaS or PaaS. This includes timing and restrictions that can have dramatic impact on the cost or flexibility of the cloud service. SAM operations can create a simple 'CSP T&C Summary' document comparing the current agreement language for the current cloud service providers in a side by side format for easy reference. This will be a great item to collaborate with the CCOE to ensure it is comprehensive and effectively highlights the key terms that can impact the team's flexibility or budget.

BYOL Use Rights Summary

SAM operations have the opportunity to create a summary of Bring Your Own License (BYOL) terms and conditions across Software Publishers and Cloud Service Providers. This intersection will aid the CCOE and IT teams in better understanding the implications of their IaaS or PaaS by CSP. Educating the teams and maintaining the currency of this document will enable SAM operations to anticipate potential areas of license non-compliance while ensuring those involved understand the impact of their selection.

BYOL License Conversion Summary

Each Software Publisher has specific language concerning the conversion or metrics by which a license will be counted when ported to an IaaS or PaaS environment. Teams need to understand that it may not be a 1 to 1 conversion and understand the multiplier, if any, they will need to account for. Again, SAM operations, who own this subject, need to be proactive and produce a central, consolidated document covering this issue and educate the teams busily identifying workloads to move to the cloud and understand the license consumption of existing deployments.

BYOL Migration Requirements

In addition to the need to understand metrics and conversion rates, SAM operations need to pay close attention to the defined times a license can run in parallel between the on-premises and cloud. Failure to shut down the on-premises environment within the required time can lead to a doubling of license consumption. SAM leaders need to craft a simple table to track the number of days software publishers allow parallel license consumption with the requirement that the day the cloud environment is established is formally documented so the period of time can be actively measured. By doing so, all are aware of timing and the potential impact if environments are not properly taken offline.

In addition, it is important to document any rules about the use of BYOL to transition to the cloud as well as reclaim or pull the license out of the cloud. Rules vary by software publisher and CSP so SAM operations have a natural opportunity to assume this responsibility and extend value to the CCOE as well as prevent unnecessary budget impact.

SaaS License Metric Summary

SAM leaders also have the opportunity to produce a central document listing license metrics and calculation approach for all identified SaaS providers in the environment. SaaS organizations continue to push past simple user or employee-based metrics. SAM leaders have the opportunity to centralize the information and produce a valuable summary to support ongoing optimization and efficiency.

Cloud Consumption Management

This is the single greatest opportunity for SAM leaders to be a crucial component of the CCOE and bring real value in the form of proactive cloud governance. Gartner has done an excellent job framing the issue of 'toxic cloud provisioning' and awareness of this dynamic is growing quickly as cloud expenditure far exceeds expectation. As covered in the preceding section on management of migrations, accelerated cloud spend combined with on premise environment cost remaining flat, a double impact to IT budgets occurs.

To effectively execute this important analysis on a monthly basis, SAM operations will need to have access to all CSP portals. The individual who conducts this analysis for SAM operations should have good familiarity with the CSP agreements, a view to recent purchases as well as any workload terminations (hopefully reflected in ITSM). The primary focus is to identify utilization along a select few dimensions in order to help IT executives quickly spot efficiency opportunities by business unit, service area, or other aspect that makes sense for the business.

As mentioned earlier, many of these core utilization elements are not consistently reported or effectively tracked by the CCOE. Understandably, the focus of the CCOE is on transitioning workload safely to achieve targeted cloud usage. Using BYOL and SaaS subscription optimization as the bridge to be proactively engaged in cloud governance, SAM operations has a strong opportunity to provide value. By doing so, SAM operations will quickly assume a leadership role in cloud governance.

Workload Utilization by CSP by month

This is a great opportunity to develop analysis that brings true insight to the business and IT to understand any variances and trending by cloud service provider.

Workload Utilization by Business Unit by month

A great way to identify ALL cloud use by business unit and perhaps even down to the cost center. Understanding utilization will show the discipline of various internal teams in managing cloud capacity while creating a platform for accurate charge-back opportunities. This is intended to be a full roll-up of all cloud utilization.

Total Workload by CSP by Business Unit by month

The first two utilization targets enable SAM operations to show trend spend and utilization by business unit by CSP. Utilization by month overlaid with growth per month enables accurate forecasting to facilitate detailed discussions based on fact. Analysis should document the current and projected financial impact of current utilization levels with variances by target utilization improvement.

Subscription Analysis

The SAM Leader Survival Guide has separated the analysis of SaaS subscription levels from the other cloud utilization as this is a critical area that receives limited focus. It is well documented by Gartner and other analysts that the shift to SaaS subscription models has enabled software publishers to increase the revenue per client while at the same time limiting incremental expense associated with providing services. This dual-impact is enabled by a client's inability to effectively track subscriptions and continually revise and update the number of subscribers for maximum efficiency.

SAM leaders have a significant opportunity in this area. CCOE's appear to pay less attention to SaaS utilization when compared to IaaS and PaaS. In some respects, SaaS is largely aligned to shadow IT or as the responsibility of the individual business unit. SAM operations have the opportunity to leverage their experience with user-based license metrics and leverage that into taking on the role of maintaining accurate utilization levels.

Part 6 – Cloud: The Future is Here – Summary

This section on the impact of Cloud on SAM operations is not intended to be an exhaustive, comprehensive, coverage on this important subject. There is a great deal more that can be covered; however, SAM professionals need to first establish a basic foundation of effective SAM operations before pushing into the cloud governance discussion. With effective implementation of the concepts outlined previously, SAM leaders have the opportunity to be a central member of the CCOE and engage in cloud governance in a meaningful fashion.

Part 7 – On the Horizon

Before we bring *The SAM Leader Survival Guide* to a close, it is important to note there are emerging technologies on the horizon that have the potential for a profound impact to software asset and IT asset management professionals. SAM leaders need to quickly establish productive operations and become engaged in cloud governance before these emerging technologies become mainstream. If not, SAM operations will lose relevance.

Technology organizations, in pursuit of supporting digital transformation, continue to adopt agile methodologies for increased speed of development and deployment. What has emerged can be referred to as microservice architecture that offers increased portability, speed and resilience. It has also produced a highly transient aspect making it very difficult to assess deployment as these elements are spun-up and spun-down dynamically.

Containers

It has been described to *The SAM Leader Survival Guide* that 'containers' are in essence the next generation of virtualization. A container approach features a shared host Operating System (OS) that improves resource utilization. Software publishers have not as yet defined how they will apply license metrics to container utilization, but if each individual guest or host OS is viewed as a core and software publishers maintain their current minimum core requirements, license consumption will have a dramatic impact.

Serverless

Cloud providers have begun to introduce the concept of 'functions' providing smaller, faster, more agile capabilities. CSPs are developing consumption plans based on 'per-second' use of resources including virtual CPUs with storage and networking separate. In some respects, this has the potential to present SAM professionals and CCOE's the challenge of measuring metrics within metrics due to the nature of functions and the linkage of multiple capabilities within the so-called function.

There is much unknown on these two topics. *The SAM Leader Survival Guide* simply wanted to bring awareness and recognize these as future issues that will have potential impact to SAM and ITAM professionals. SAM leaders should remain focused on core activities to establish SAM operations while building the bridge to participate and contribute in effective cloud governance and while maintaining awareness for any internal use of containers or serverless capabilities within the organization.

Part 8 – Pulling It All Together

We recognize *that The SAM Leader Survival Guide* has provided a long list of actions and tactics for SAM leaders to achieve enhanced performance and that it will be impractical to implement everything at once. Items may make no sense to address today, but over the coming months, an internal event may occur triggering potential inclusion in your strategy. Our goal was to provide a reference that can be reviewed by SAM professionals ongoing as they mature their organization and seek additional means to provide value.

SAM professionals have the opportunity to use the recommendations contained within the SAM Leader Survival Guide and map a phased approach to implementation of operational improvements. Consider identifying four phases with Phase 1 (months 1-6), Phase 2 (months 7-12), Phase 3 (+12 months) and Phase 4 being those items or activities you do not believe applicable to your operations. This will enable you to create a SAM operational roadmap of the elements you wish to deploy and when. It is important to not overwhelm your sponsors and stakeholders but at the same time, establish a momentum that will help you establish SAM operations as the strategic partner appropriate for your organization.

Once this has been completed, look at each of the items by phase and prioritize implementation of the items so there is a natural, logical, sequence to achieving your goal for that specific phase.

By taking this action, you have converted *The SAM Leader Survival Guide* into an actionable game plan that we are confident will deliver positive results for you, your team and your organization.

We wish you continued success in your software asset management career.

List of Acronyms

ART	Audit Response Team
BA	Business Analyst
BAU	Business as Usual
BRM	Business Relationship Manager
BYOL	Bring Your Own License
CAM	Cloud Asset Management
CCOE	Cloud Center of Excellence
CFO	Chief Financial Officer
CI	Configuration Item
CIO	Chief Information Officer
CISO	Chief Information Security Officer
CMDB	Configuration Management Database
CPO	Chief Procurement Officer
CSP	Cloud Service Provider
CTB	Change the Business
EA	Enterprise Agreement
ELP	Effective License Position
HAM	Hardware Asset Management
IaaS	Infrastructure as a Service
IAITAM	International Association of IT Asset Management
ILMT	IBM License Metric Tool

InfoSecInformation Security

ISO	International Organization for Standardization
ITAM	Information Technology Asset Management
ITIL	Information Technology Infrastructure Library
ITSM	Information Technology Service Management
LMS	License Management Services
M&A	Mergers and Acquisitions
MAP	Microsoft Application Planning Toolkit
MSDN	Microsoft Developer Network
MOIS	Microsoft-Oracle-IBM-SAP
NDA	Non-disclosure Agreement
OS	Operating System
PaaS	Platform as a Service
PMO	Project Management Organization
POC	Proof of Concept
PVU	Processor Value Unit
RoE	Rules of Engagement
ROI	Return on Investment
RTB	Run the Business
SaaS	Software as a Service
SCCM	System Center Configuration Manager
SLA	Service Level Agreement
T&C	Terms and Conditions

TEM	Telecom Expense Management
ULA	Unlimited License Agreement
VMO	Vendor Management Office

About the Author

Jim Hussey is the former leader of a Fortune 500 technology vendor management organization. In this role, he was given the responsibility to build a SAM operation due to the significant negative outcome of a software audit. Through this experience, Jim learned firsthand the challenges and obstacles SAM professionals encounter as they attempt to implement the software asset discipline.

Upon leaving the organization in which he implemented a robust SAM discovery capability combined with a global team of SAM analysts, Jim began a detailed study of the software asset management community. The goal was to identify best practices and uncover valuable lessons learned that others could benefit from. Utilizing his background as a journalist and researcher, in addition to authoring *The SAM Leader Survival Guide*, Jim is active in developing SAM market specific research to provide SAM professionals independent data to develop SAM strategy.

Jim is a frequent blogger on the subject of SAM leadership coaching and professional development, a member of sammaturity.com's content development team and lead contributor to sammaturity's SAM professional development certification programs.

Currently the leader of NPI's SAM practice providing clients SAM advisory and audit support services, Jim continues efforts to support SAM professionals in achieving greater results and career satisfaction.

CPSIA information can be obtained
at www.ICGtesting.com
Printed in the USA
LVHW031553230520
656343LV00006B/413